HISTORY OF THE 5th BATTALION 13th FRONTIER FORCE RIFLES

COLONEL H. C. WYLLY, C.B.

The Naval & Military Press Ltd

Published by
The Naval & Military Press Ltd
5 Riverside, Brambleside, Bellbrook
Industrial Estate, Uckfield, East Sussex,
TN22 1QQ England
Tel: +44 (0) 1825 749494
Fax: +44 (0) 1825 765701
www.naval-military-press.com

GENERAL SIR J. L. VAUGHAN, K.C.B.

HISTORY of THE 5th BATTALION 13th FRONTIER FORCE RIFLES 1849-1926

By

COLONEL H. C. WYLLY, C.B.

1929

CONTENTS

CHAPTER I.

FIRST PERIOD : 1849—1881. PAGES

The Punjab in 1849. The Raising and Composition of a new Military Force for internal security and guarding of the Frontier. Creation of the 5th Punjab Infantry. "The Punjab Irregular Force." The Wardenship of the Marches. The Regiment volunteers for service in the Second Burmese War. The outbreak of the great Mutiny. The 5th ordered to Attock—to Mardan—to Lucknow. Joins a force under General Sir Hope Grant. Operations in Oude and on the Nepal Border. Return to the Punjab. Transfer of the Government of India by the East India Company to the Crown. Introduction of the Staff Corps. Issue of the first Royal War Medal for service in the Mutiny. The Ambeyla Campaign. Regiment re-armed with the Enfield Rifle. Issue of the Indian General Service Medal. "Punjab Frontier Force." Operations against the Jawaki Afridis. Opening of the Second Afghan War. Regiment joins the Kurram Valley Field Force. Engaged at the Peiwar Kotal, at Charasia, at Deh-Afghana, in the defence of Sherpur Cantonment. Issue of medals for Second Afghan War. Award of Battle Honours 1–44

CHAPTER II.

SECOND PERIOD : 1881—1914.

Operations against the Mahsuds. Survey work in the Takht-i-Suliman. Mobilization for possible war with Russia. Punjab Frontier Force placed under the Commander-in-Chief in India. Army manœuvres at Attock. Regiment takes part in the Miranzai Expedition of 1891. Re-armament with Martini-Henry rifles. Trouble threatened with Afghanistan. Operations on the Samana. Opening of the Tirah Expedition of 1897. Reasons for non-employment of Regiments enlisting Afridis. Blockade of the Mahsuds. Reorganization by Lord Kitchener of the Indian Army. Punjab Frontier Force ceases to exist as a separate body. Re-numbering of all Indian regiments. "5th Punjab Infantry" becomes "58th Vaughan's Rifles (Frontier Force)." Regiment proceeds to Quetta. The Great War. Causes of the outbreak. The Indian Contingent for service in Europe. Regiment ordered to join the 7th (Meerut) Division. The 58th Rifles sail from Karachi for "an unknown destination"... 45–66

CHAPTER III.

THIRD PERIOD : 1914—1920.

The Voyage to France. Arrival at Marseilles. 58th moves up to the Front. In action near Festubert. Death of Lieut.-Colonel Venour. The Battle of Festubert. The Winter in France. Arrival of Reinforcements. The Battle of Neuve Chapelle. The Battle of Aubers Ridge. Casualties and strengths. Death of Lieut.-Colonel Davidson-Houston. Givenchy. The Indian Corps leaves France. 58th embarks at Marseilles for Egypt. Service on the Suez Canal. 58th ordered to the Palestine Front. Joins the 234th Brigade of the 75th Division. The capture and occupation of Jerusalem. Operations at the Latrun Pass. 75th Division joins the XXIst Corps. The Coastal Advance. Operations at El Kefr village. Attack on the Tabsor Defences. End of the Turkish opposition. 58th returns to Egypt. Employed in maintaining internal quiet. Party of Indian ranks sent to England. Ordered to embark for India. Regiment sails from Suez. Disembarkation at Karachi. Arrival at Multan 67–88

CHAPTER IV.

Fourth Period : 1920—1926.

PAGES

The North-West Frontier. Trouble with Afghanistan. Affairs in Waziristan. 58th ordered to assist in the blockade of the Wazirs. The Muhajerin movement. Occupation of Wana. Opposition experienced. Reorganization of the Indian Army. Grouping of Infantry Regiments. Regiment to be the 4th Battalion of 13th Group. Regiment is withdrawn from Wana. Complimentary Orders. Honours and rewards. Title again changed to 5th Bn. 13th Frontier Force Rifles (Vaughan's). Composition of Group. Unveiling of Punjab Frontier Force Memorial at Kohat. Memorial Tablet in Kohat Church. Honours and rewards. Macgregor Memorial Medal. Regiment moves to Abbottabad 89–111

APPENDICES.

PAGE

A.—The Great War. British and Indian Officers and other ranks killed and wounded 115

B.—Honours and Awards gained during the war (1914-18), by the 58th Rifles ... 118

C.—List of Units from which reinforcements were received 121

D.—The Work of the Depot 121

E.—Roll of Officers of the 5th Punjab Infantry, 58th Frontier Force Rifles, and 5th Battalion 13th Frontier Force Rifles (1849—1926) 122

ILLUSTRATIONS

General Sir J. L. Vaughan, K.C.B. ... ... *Frontispiece*

FACING PAGE

Captain J. E. Gastrell 6

General Sir J. W. McQueen, G.C.B. 36

5th P.I. Defences, Sherpur, 1880 42

British and Indian Officers, 5th P.I., 1889 42

N.C.Os. and Men, 5th P.I., 1889 48

Indian Officers, 5th P.I., 1893 48

British Officers, 58th (Vaughan's) Rifles (F.F.), 1912 66

British Officers, 58th (Vaughan's) Rifles (F.F.), Waziristan, 1921 66

Survivors of 1914-15, Thal, 1926 88

British and Indian Officers, Past and Present, Thal, 1926 88

Wana Keep, 1920 103

13th Frontier Force Rifles, Reunion, Abbottabad, 1927 103

MAPS

Engagement of 23rd November, 1914 ... ...

Action of 20th-22nd December, 1914 ... ...

Action of 25th September, 1915 ... ...

Battle for Mesmiyeh ... ...

Action at Tabsor ... ...

North-West Frontier ... ...

} at End of Book

REGIMENTAL HISTORY

OF THE

5th BATTALION
13th FRONTIER FORCE RIFLES

CHAPTER I

First Period

1849—1881

The battle of Gujerat, fought on February 21st, 1849, brought to an end the second of the two wars with the Sikhs, and on April 2nd of the same year the Punjab was annexed.

For the government of the new Province, including the Jullundur Doab, previously annexed, and the Cis-Sutlej States, a Board of Administration was appointed consisting of three members—the brothers Lawrence, John and Henry, and Mr. Charles Greville Mansei. The three members had equal responsibility, but each had also his own department ; " Mr. Mansel, as a trained civilian from a Regulation Province, smoothly and effectively organized the judicial administration of the Punjab. John Lawrence, as a strenuous revenue officer, re-settled the land-tax and fiscal system on a basis at once more favourable to the people and more profitable to the Government. Sir Henry Lawrence, as a soldier-political, was charged more directly with the military defence and our relations towards the lately subdued Chiefs and Sikh fief-holders. He also presided as head of the Board."*

Having arranged for the civil administration of the new Province. Lord Dalhousie, the Governor-General, now turned his attention to

* Hunter, " The Marquess of Dalhousie," p. 94.

the nature and size of the military force which should be maintained for its internal security and the guarding of its frontiers, and in regard to these matters he had to consider the position which existed previous to and at the time of annexation. To use his own words in explanation of the action which he took : " With the sanction of the President, Edwardes, Taylor, Abbott and George Lawrence, who were detached during the troubles of last year, raised levies to protect themselves and preserve, if possible, their hold of the country. Some of the Durbar Regiments remained faithful also. To the whole of these Regiments service hereafter was guaranteed. To many of the levies service was either positively or constructively promised. Much as I disliked it, the promise having been made, I felt that good faith must be kept, and I confirmed the promise. The officers of the Army and the newspapers object. Their cue is to urge the necessity of an increase to the regular regiments of the Line. Thence would result large promotion. Others object to these corps from the nature of them, and of these objectors is the new Commander-in-Chief." (General Sir Charles Napier.) " Most people object from the erroneous idea that they are Sikh corps. They are nothing of the sort. I have prohibited more than one-tenth being Sikhs, which will keep the total number of Sikhs in the five regiments to 400."*

In a letter dated Lahore, April 17th, 1849, from the Secretary to the Board of Administration to the Secretary to the Government of India, the following appears under the heading of " Instructions for the guidance of all officers raising Cavalry and Infantry Regiments of Irregulars in the Punjab " :—

" 1. The object to be kept in view is the absorption (as far as consistent with efficiency) of the Irregular partisan levies raised during the late war, as well as such other troops, whether regular or irregular, as may have remained faithful throughout the insurrection.

" 2. The following proportions should as much as possible be adhered to in the several regiments :—

" One-fourth Sikhs selected by preference from the Lahore cavalry and infantry services who remained faithful.

* Lee-Warner, "The Life of the Marquis of Dalhousie," Vol. I, p. 260.

"One half Punjabees of any other class or section—*i.e.*, natives of the countries, hill or plain, trans-Sutlej, not Sikhs.

"One quarter Hindoostanees.

"3. Recruiting officers will not be so particular as to the size, appearance or age of the candidates for enlistment, as if raising corps in more peaceful times in the Provinces; as it is at this moment as essential to provide a livelihood for those soldiers of the Maharajah who have not forfeited their claims, as it is to obtain for our own Government a force for the protection of the new territory. Any soldier, therefore, who is efficient and able to perform active duty should be considered eligible, whether he be smart-looking or otherwise.

"4. The sanction of Government has been solicited for Commanding Officers to select a proportion of smart and experienced Native Officers and men from corps of the Line, which, if obtained, will be communicated to Commanding Officers without delay.

"5. Many Native Officers of the Sikh service will be found among the candidates for enlistment, perhaps more than there will be vacancies for in the new regiments, but the claims of all should be considered with reference to their former standing and condition.

"6. The pay of the Sowars in the Cavalry will be Rs.20 per mensem, that of the Infantry Rs.7; no batta will be given to either in any situation or place, but the baggage of the Infantry to a reasonable extent, which will be hereafter set forth, in a scale according to rank, will be carried at the expense of Government. The pay of Native Officers will be in proportion to that of their men and will be notified when fixed by Government.

"7. The Corps of Cavalry and Infantry will be raised at the following places, and Commanding Officers are called upon to proceed to their depots forthwith:—

"Peshawar	1st Cavalry	and	1st Infantry.
Rawal Pindi	2nd	,,	,, 3rd	,,
Lahore	3rd	,,	,, 4th	,,
Pind Dadun Khan	4th	,,	,, 2nd	,,
Mooltan and Dera Ismail Khan	5th	,,	,, 5th	,,

"8. Commanding Officers will report the progress of their enlistment weekly for the Board's information, distinguishing the number of men recruited of each of the three classes specified in paragraph 2, as also men previously in service, from those men enlisted for the first time."

The Secretary to the Government of India replied to this in letter No. 715 of May 16th, stating that the Governor-General had expressed his general approval of these instructions, but that the new Corps should not be called "The Punjab Contingent," as appears to have originally been suggested, but the 1st to the 5th Punjab Cavalry and the 1st to the 5th Punjab Infantry; and, further, that baggage would not be carried at Government expense. The composition of the regiments of each arm was then laid down, and it was decreed that each infantry regiment should be composed of eight companies, each having one subadar, one jemadar, five naiks, two drummers and 100 sepoys, with, for each battalion, one European Commandant, one European Second-in-Command, one European Adjutant and one European Medical Officer. There were also not to be more than ten Sikhs in any company.

The following is the text of the final order on the subject of the new corps:—

"No. 754.

"General Order by the Right Honourable the Governor-General of India.

"India,

"Foreign Department, Simla, *May* 18*th*, 1849.

"The Right Honourable the Governor-General is pleased to direct that five regiments of cavalry and five regiments of infantry shall be raised within the Punjaub, according to instructions issued to the Board of Administration.

"The Governor-General is pleased to make the following appointments accordingly:—

* * * * *

"5TH REGIMENT PUNJAUB INFANTRY.

"Lieutenant J. E. Gastrell, 13th Native Infantry, Commandant.

"Lieutenant G. W. G. Green, 2nd Bengal European Regiment, Second-in-Command.

"Lieutenant W. McNeile, 5th Native Infantry, Adjutant.

"Apothecary Thomas Nulty.

"By Order of the Right Honourable the Governor-General of India.

(Sd.) "H. M. ELLIOTT.
"*Secy. to the Government of India with the Governor-General.*

(Sd.) "J. STUART, Colonel.
"*Secy. to the Government of India, Mily. Dept., with the Governor-General.*"

The 5th Punjab Infantry was not, as in the first instance ordered, raised at Dera Ismail Khan, but at Leiah in the Mianwali District, about midway between Dera Ismail and Dera Ghazi Khan; and by March, 1850, the Regiment, being completed and armed, was brought on to the roster of garrison duty, when the detachment of a regiment of the Line, which had hitherto taken all the duties of the station, was withdrawn.

In the following month the 5th Punjab Infantry marched from Leiah to Dera Ghazi Khan, whence two companies were detached, the one to Mithankote and the other to Jhung, this last detachment not rejoining Headquarters until May, 1851.

In November, 1850, the composition of the Regiment was as follows :—

Sikhs	86 all ranks.
Other Punjabis	454 „ „
Hindustanis...	360 „ „
Making a total of	900 „ „

but early in the new year two important orders were published, slightly altering the composition of the new regiments and bestowing upon them a new designation.

General Order No. 577 of February 15th, 1851, finally laid down that the corps raised in 1849 should be called "the Punjab Irregular Force," and that it should consist of three light field batteries of artillery, five regiments of cavalry and five regiments of infantry, "for general service in the Punjab and the Trans-Indus Provinces under British rule, as well as beyond these limits should the exigencies of the Service require it." The Force to be commanded by a Brigadier at a consolidated salary of Rs.2000 per mensem.

The establishment of each infantry regiment was now to be :— 1 Commandant, 1 Second-in-Command, 1 Adjutant and Quartermaster, 1 Apothecary, 1 Sergeant-Major, 1 Quartermaster-Sergeant, 2 native doctors, 8 subadars, 8 jemadars, 48 havildars, 48 naiks, 17 drummers and 800 sepoys.

Then a few days later, on February 26th, General Order No. 608 sanctions the establishment of Sikhs per infantry regiment being raised to 200.

The first Brigadier to be appointed Commandant of the Punjab Irregular Force was Brigadier J. S. Hodgson, of the 12th Bengal Native Infantry, in which regiment he held at the time the rank of Captain only; Captain W. R. Prout, 56th Bengal Native Infantry, was his Brigade Major.

The Regiment had been just under a year at Dera Ghazi Khan when, in May, 1851, the Left Wing, under Lieutenant Green, was ordered to proceed to Asni; but previous to this the command of the Regiment had already changed hands, for General Orders of February 4th contain the following announcement under date of the 1st of that month :—"5th Infantry, Punjab Irregular Force, Captain R. Drew, of the 45th Madras Native Infantry, to be Commandant *vice* Captain J. E. Gastrell, placed at the disposal of H.E. the Commander-in-Chief."

Up to January, 1852, the 5th Punjab Infantry had been dressed and equipped like the Line regiments of the Bengal Army, except that the rank and file wore the black leather cross-belts of the kind issued to local corps. But in this month some changes were inaugurated, the white linen jackets and trousers in particular, which were provided for wear in the hot weather, being found quite unsuited for a regiment engaged in the rough duties of the Derajat frontier. A dyed linen

CAPTAIN J. E. GASTRELL

jacket and trousers were therefore substituted, and each man was further required to keep up a khaki smock and pyjamas for service and fatigue duties.

At this time both Captain Drew and the officer who had been detailed to officiate as Commandant in his absence, appear to have been away on leave, and Captain J. L. Vaughan, of the 2nd Punjab Infantry, was appointed officiating Commandant, the appointment being confirmed on October 22nd, 1852.

In March, 1852, a line of posts having been established along the North-West Frontier, the Regiment was called upon to furnish infantry detachments at no fewer than sixteen different posts from Kin to Vihowah, a distance of 200 miles. This duty, though harassing and uninteresting, afforded a useful training to the non-commissioned officers and men, particularly to the former, and gave them an insight into their duties and responsibilities, the benefit of which has been of an enduring character in the carrying out of the Wardenship of the frontier, which, since the annexation of the Punjab, had become our troublous heritage.

On March 16th, 1852, one Yusaf Khan, a chief of the Kasranis, a Baluch tribe inhabiting the extreme north of the Dera Ghazi Khan district, a portion of the south of the Dera Ismail Khan district and the hills to the west of these tracts, organized a raid against Dera Fateh Khan, twenty miles from the hills, plundered the bazaar and carried off a good deal of cattle, being followed up on his retirement by some sabres of the 1st Punjab Cavalry and nearly a hundred men of the local levies. Assistance being called for, No. 5 Company of the Regiment, which was then on detachment at Mangrotah, marched at once on Vihowah, and, under Subadar Umrao Misser, accomplished the march of thirty miles during the night by bad roads and in heavy rain. After a day's halt at Vihowah the company returned to Dera Ghazi Khan, ninety-six miles, in three marches, accompanying Sir Henry Lawrence, the President of the Board of Administration, who was at the time on tour in the district. In the same month Sir Henry inspected the Headquarters of the 5th Punjab Infantry.

About this time the transport, enabling Frontier corps to march out under active service conditions at the very shortest notice, was completed, the establishment being seventy camels and forty mules. The former were purchased for the most part in the Dera Ghazi Khan district, the mules coming mainly from the neighbourhood of Jhelum and Rawal Pindi, a few being obtained in Upper Scinde.

The terms of the treaty concluded after the first Burmese War of 1824-26 with the King of Ava, had never been observed either by that potentate himself or by his successor, and the Government of India, in the years that immediately followed, had been too much occupied with the Afghan War, the brief Gwalior campaign and the two wars with the Sikhs, properly to look into matters. By 1851, however, peace conditions were once again prevailing on and within the frontiers of British India, and Lord Dalhousie began to give ear to the recital of the grievances of British merchants trading with Burma, and fresh negotiations were opened. To these the Burmese authorities replied only with insolence and evasions, and in April, 1852, the second Burmese War commenced. The initial operations were considerably protracted and there was a good deal of sickness among the troops detailed for the expeditionary force; whereupon, it seeming by no means unlikely that additional regiments might be needed, the 5th Punjab Infantry volunteered to a man in May, 1852, for service in Burma. The offer was acknowledged by the Governor-General in the following gratifying terms :—

"*The Governor-General has perused with great satisfaction the account of this manifestation of loyal and soldierlike feeling on the part of the men, but His Lordship in Council is precluded, on account of the distance at which they are placed and the frontier on which they are engaged, from employing them in Burma.*"

In August of this year the first set of Colours was received and was presented to the Regiment.

General Sir J. L. Vaughan, who at this time as a captain was Commandant of the 5th Punjab Infantry, has stated* that in those days "the different classes of which the Regiment was composed were mixed up in the ranks, every class being represented in the same company. . . . One of the earliest reforms I introduced was to form

* "My Service in the Indian Army—and After," pp. 44, 45.

the Regiment in class companies, and the 5th eventually stood as follows :—

" 2	Companies	Sikhs.
2	,,	Punjab Mahammedans.
2	,,	Pathans.
1	Company	Dogras.
1	,,	Mixed."

In February, 1853, orders were received for changing the full dress uniform of the Regiment from red to khaki or drab.

During the months of April to June of this year there occurred some of those minor disturbances on the frontier, for which the regiments of the Punjab Irregular Force had always to be prepared, and which their readiness and initiative frequently prevented from assuming more serious proportions, necessitating the employment of large punitive forces.

During the months of April and May Jemadar Sohan Tewary was commanding the outpost at Mahoi, one of the three passes—the Vihowah and the Sangarh being the other two—which lead from the Bozdar country into the plains, when a party of marauders came down and carried off cattle from the neighbouring villages ; the jemadar at once turned out his men, pursued the party and succeeded in recovering all the cattle which they had driven off.

Again, in June, the threatening attitude of the Marris, described by Paget and Mason as " the most powerful and the most troublesome of all the Biluch tribes," and as having a fighting strength of 3,000, caused orders to be issued for the prompt dispatch of an additional company of the Regiment to Asni ; it marched from Dera Ghazi Khan at 9 p.m. one day and accomplished the journey to Asni in three marches, the distance being ninety-six miles.

During July the Regiment was employed on several occasions, on the requisition of the Civil authorities, in repairing and strengthening the *bunds* in the vicinity of the town and cantonment of Dera Ghazi Khan, consequent on the overflowing of the Indus, the thanks of the Government being afterwards accorded to the Regiment for the zealous and efficient assistance given.

At this time the composition of the 5th Punjab Infantry was as under :—

Sikhs and Punjabis	565 all ranks.
Hindustanis...	246 „ „
Trans-Indus men	95 „ „
	906 „ „

In September and October the post of Vidor, on the frontier opposite Dera Ghazi Khan, had to be reinforced at the very shortest possible notice to meet threatened attacks by the Bozdars.

In December of this year the Headquarters and Right Wing of the Regiment marched to Bannu in course of relief, the Left Wing taking its place temporarily at Dera Ghazi Khan ; but in February, 1854, this Wing rejoined Headquarters at Bannu, when the Regiment was united for the first time since April, 1850. While quartered at Bannu, rifles (two-grooved) were received sufficient for two complete companies and were issued to the flank companies ; and at the same time the designation of "Grenadier" and "Light" companies was abolished,* and the companies were now numbered consecutively from 1 to 8.

Certain other matters of a purely regimental or domestic nature, introduced between October, 1853, and November, 1854, may here be mentioned. *Pukkalis*, one per company, were sanctioned in the place of hand *bhistis*, and it was directed that each man should be supplied with two *pakkals* for carrying a supply of water on the march. In March, 1854, two *langris* or cooks were added to the establishment of each company, and about the same time *puggris* were substituted for the Kilmarnock caps which had hitherto been worn throughout the Indian Army, similar to those in use in the British Service. Finally, in November, each man was provided with a *poshtin* at a cost of Rs.2 as.2 for each non-commissioned officer and sepoy and Rs.10 for each Indian officer.

On December 13th, 1854, Lord Dalhousie nominated Major Neville Chamberlain to succeed Brigadier J. S. Hodgson in the command of

* The Indian Army in this matter was in advance of the British, in which Grenadier and Light Infantry companies were not abolished till January 29th, 1858.

the Punjab Irregular Force, with the rank of Brigadier, and on February 7th, 1855, he took over the command at Kohat, being required in the following month to lead an expeditionary force into the Miranzai Valley, when a company of the 5th Punjab Infantry was ordered to find the garrison of Latamar, some ten miles to the north-east of Bannu, while the troops from Kohat were employed in the Miranzai Valley; this company rejoined Headquarters on May 31st.

In June the composition of the different classes composing the Regiment was as follows :—

Sikhs and Punjabis	548	all	ranks.
Hindustanis...	222	,,	,,
Trans-Indus men	157	,,	,,
	927	,,	,,

"In the autumn of 1855 Brigadier Chamberlain had to make another expedition in order to punish the Urakzais, a large and warlike tribe lying between the Afridis and the Waziris. On August 25th a force, consisting of the Peshawar Mountain Train Battery (four guns), No. 3 Punjab Light Field Battery (five guns), 4th Punjab Cavalry, 1st, 2nd and 3rd Punjab Infantry, was assembled at Hangu, a valley to the south-west of Kohat."* To facilitate the movements of this force the 5th Punjab Infantry was ordered at a moment's notice to send three companies to garrison Latamar, Bahadur Khel and Nari, respectively, in relief of the 3rd Punjab Infantry. This order was received at 11 a.m., the detachment marched at noon, reached Latamar (19 miles) the same evening, and Bahadur Khel, without any halt, at 11 p.m. The remaining company marched on to Nari the following morning and reached that place, thirteen miles distant, some hours before noon. Subadar Mian Singh was in command of the three companies. No wonder that of such leaders General Vaughan wrote :—"The good quality and efficiency of the Native Officers became a marked feature of the Force. They commanded their troops and companies as well in the field as in quarters, and their opinion and advice were constantly asked by their commanding officers on all occasions of difficulty."

* Forrest, "Life of Field-Marshal Sir Neville Chamberlain," p. 308.

In April, 1856, the Regiment was inspected by Brigadier N. Chamberlain, commanding the Punjab Irregular Force.

Again certain minor matters of interior economy should be mentioned, which came into existence in the autumn of this year. In August a Native Adjutant was sanctioned, and Jemadar Gunga Dubi was appointed to the post; in the same month the Regiment was authorized to enlist twenty-five recruits in excess of establishment on a subsistence allowance of Rs.3 a month per man; and in September a third company—No. 4—was completely re-armed with the two-grooved rifle already mentioned;* while by February of the year following, 251 more rifles having been received, it was found possible to issue them to Nos. 2 and 7 Companies and partially to re-arm No. 3. In the whole Regiment 587 men were by that date thus armed.

In September, 1856, the outpost of Latamar was transferred from the Kohat to the Bannu district, when the Regiment was ordered to find its garrison; and in October the 5th, having been placed under orders to proceed to Kohat on relief, 210 non-commissioned officers and men marched to Bahadur Khel and Nari and took over those posts. While in command at Bahadur Khel, Subadar Sohan Tewary again distinguished himself by surprising a party of salt smugglers and capturing all their cattle; the drovers would also probably have fallen into his hands had they not been alarmed by the accidental discharge of a firearm.

In October the Headquarters marched to Kohat, followed a few days after by the rest of the Regiment under Lieutenant J. B. Lind; but two months later this officer proceeded with No. 1 and No. 8 Companies—strength, 4 Indian officers and 188 other ranks—to join a force of close upon 5,000 men and 14 guns which, under Brigadier Chamberlain, was ordered to the Miranzai Valley to bring to terms the Turis, a tribe inhabiting the Kurram Valley, who, from the date of our annexation of the Kohat district, had given us considerable trouble, and were already this year guilty of carrying out no fewer than thirteen raids across our border. The Turis submitted before this display of force, and on the last day of December Chamberlain's troops returned to Kohat and dispersed, Lieutenant Lind marching his two companies

* This would seem to have been the Brunswick rifle, introduced at home in 1836.

back to Headquarters. Here Lieutenant J. Williamson had been in command of what had remained behind of the Regiment—viz., 507 of all ranks—while 210 were on outpost duties and 211 were on command; but as many men at Headquarters were sickly, and the guard and escort duty was heavy, the few healthy men were very hard worked during the absence of the Miranzai Field Force.

By January, 1857, the composition of the Regiment was as under :—

Punjabis	470	all ranks.
Trans-Indus men	210	„ „
Hindustanis	170	„ „
Cis-Sutlej men	78	„ „
	928	„ „

Of these 928 Indian officers, non-commissioned officers and men, 551 were Mahammedans, while the remaining 377 were Sikhs and Hindus.

By the beginning of the year 1857 the 5th Punjab Infantry had been close upon eight years in existence, and although up to this date the Regiment had never had the good fortune to be actively engaged with an enemy, yet it had borne a very large share in the heavy and unceasing duties of the Trans-Indus frontier, having at different times served at every station from Asni to Kohat, and furnished garrisons for every single outpost on the whole border line. The severity of the duty devolving upon the Regiment, when distributed between Dera Ghazi Khan and Asni in particular, was such that in 1853 the furlough due to the men had to be partially withheld, but no murmur of any kind was ever heard, while the Regiment was singularly free from crime. The time was now, however, approaching when the 5th Punjab Infantry was to be called upon to take part in very serious and protracted operations in the field, and at the outset in a terrain and under conditions of service altogether different from those to which the regiments of the Punjab Irregular Force were accustomed, and for which they had originally been called into existence.

Early in this year there appears to have been some idea of sending a punitive expedition into the country of the Waziris, and on March

18th the Headquarters and five companies were warned to march on the 18th to Dera Ismail Khan with a view to joining the force; but in the end Brigadier Chamberlain came to the conclusion that the time for such an expedition was not propitious, and, John Lawrence agreeing with him, the project was for the present abandoned.

On May 1st, 1857, three companies were detached to take over the outposts at Bahadur Khel and Nari.

The causes of the Great Mutiny which broke out in this month have been described in very many histories, and it would seem to be somewhat out of place to retail these afresh and at any length in a purely regimental record. But the following should be said in partial explanation of all that in the spring of the year 1857 came to pass.

The regular Bengal Infantry regiments numbered seventy-four at this date, nearly all recruited from Oude or from the North-West Province; recent wars had brought the Indian Army up to an abnormal strength, outnumbering the British garrison by nearly five to one; while the British regiments were so scattered that any combined action was difficult, if not indeed wellnigh impossible, and the few railways made rapid concentration out of the question. Succeeding years of mismanagement and indifferent administration, as also injudicious curtailment of the powers of commanding officers of Indian regiments, had greatly weakened the bonds of discipline in the Bengal Army, and many of the sepoys were in a restless, suspicious frame of mind, only too ready to hearken to the preachings of the disaffected. There had not been wanting in the past warnings that discontent existed in the ranks; as far back as 1849 Sir Charles Napier had declared that "a mutiny with the sepoys is the most formidable danger menacing our Indian Empire"; while Chamberlain equally foresaw the coming danger, stating that "if the bonds of discipline are not firmly and justly held, the mighty host will turn and rend us."

All that was needed to provoke the actual outbreak was an excuse, and this was forthcoming in the agitation, on religious and caste grounds, against the "greased cartridge" used with the new Enfield rifle, with which at this time it had been decided to re-arm the infantry regiments of the Bengal Army.

In January and early in March there were serious outbreaks of disaffection among the troops quartered at Berhampore and Barrackpore in Lower Bengal, and it was thought that the disbanding of the regiments concerned had put an end to the mutinous spirit which was abroad ; but on Sunday, May 10th, the Indian regiments stationed at Meerut revolted, murdered many of their British officers and took the road to Delhi, on arrival at which city they demanded that the old King, Bahadur Shah, should reseat himself upon the throne of the Great Mogul.

On the night of May 11th two telegrams reached Peshawar from Meerut and Delhi, the one stating that the Indian troops at that station were in open mutiny, that the cantonments had been burnt, several British officers killed, and that the British troops were defending themselves in their barracks ; while the other gave the news that the mutineers from Meerut had come over to Delhi, and had burnt the bungalows there and killed many Europeans. Then on May 12th there came from Delhi to John Lawrence, the Lieutenant-Governor* of the Punjab, then at Rawal Pindi, another telegram which ran :—" The sepoys have come in from Meerut and are burning everything. Mr. Todd is dead and we hear many Europeans. We must shut up."

A council of war was at once called together at Meerut, and it was decided to form a Mobile Column, composed of British and Punjab regiments drawn from Peshawar and Rawal Pindi, and to hold it ready at Jhelum for all possible eventualities.

On May 14th at daybreak an express was received from Brigadier Chamberlain at Peshawar, directing the 5th Punjab Infantry to march with the utmost expedition to Attock, to secure the bridge of boats over the Indus and also the Fort, at that time held by a detachment of the 55th Native Infantry, which it was considered could not be trusted in the light of recent events at Meerut and Delhi, and which it was intended should take the place at Mardan of the Corps of Guides, ordered to join the Mobile Column.

The Headquarters of the Regiment marched the same night to Gumbat, Lieutenant Lind remaining behind to meet and bring on the three companies relieved from duty at the outposts ; and, marching on by bad roads and in great heat by Shadipore and Nilabgarh, the

* The alteration of title from that of Chief Commissioner was made in March, 1856.

Headquarters reached Attock about 8 a.m. on May 18th. It was found that the bridge of boats had been dismantled for the season on the previous day, but a small party of some eighty men was passed over the river as rapidly as possible in boats, left a small guard in the Kabul gateway, and then, pushing on through the lower fort, occupied the Lahore gate also.

The guards of the 55th Native Infantry, not unreasonably under the circumstances, made some demur about handing over their charge without orders from their own Commanding Officer, who was not on the spot; but these scruples were overcome and the detachment of the 55th, taking the Peshawar road, marched off sullenly to rejoin the Headquarters of their Regiment at Mardan, leaving behind, however, a small guard on the Khyrabad side of the ferry.

On May 21st the remainder of the 5th Punjab Infantry joined under Lieutenant Lind.

That morning a loyal chief, one Fatteh Khan, Khattak, who had been charged by the Commissioner of Peshawar with the duty of guarding the further end of the ferry, had reported to Major Vaughan that sepoys of the 55th Native Infantry had made use of mutinous expressions to some of his men, and Major Vaughan at once sent orders to Lieutenant Lind, as he was about to cross, to make prisoners of these men of the 55th. The execution of this order appears to have alarmed a larger party of the same regiment on guard under a native officer in the Engineers' timber yard; and, instigated by their leader, this party got under arms and marched off towards Nowshera, threatening to fire upon Lieutenant Lind. Nearly all Lieutenant Lind's party, except some twelve men, had by this time crossed the Indus to Fort Attock, but with this small party he followed up the men of the 55th—some thirty or forty in number—and though not strong enough to attack them, he made two of them prisoners, and, by alarming the police posts along the road, got information of what had occurred conveyed to Nowshera, in time to prepare the officer commanding that station for the arrival of the men of the 55th Native Infantry.

Lieutenant Lind specially brought to notice the services of Havildar Muddeh Khan and of Privates Gudut Singh and Mir Ahmed Khan in this affair.

On the evening of May 21st instructions were received from the Lieut.-Governor for the immediate raising of four additional companies.

At 2 p.m. next day an express message was delivered from Brigadier Chamberlain directing the Regiment to march immediately to Nowshera and there attack, if necessary, a portion of the 55th said to have broken out into mutiny. The 5th set off at dusk,* crossing the Indus with some difficulty owing to a violent storm. "That night march," says General Vaughan in his autobiography, "remains in my memory as the most fatiguing I ever made. The distance to the rendezvous was about twenty-five miles, with the Kabul River to cross at the sixteenth. The heat was, of course, excessive. The marches from Kohat to Attock, though only four, had been long and rough, and were performed during the usual hours of sleep. The time was one of intense excitement. All these causes combined to make this long night march unusually trying. To add to it all, we fully expected to find Nowshera in the hands of the mutinous sepoys, and that our further march would be opposed by them." Nowshera was reached at daybreak on the 23rd, when it was learnt that the 55th had for the most part returned to their duty and had been marched off to Mardan to join the Headquarters of the Regiment.

The 5th Punjab Infantry now occupied quarters in the British Infantry Barracks so as to be at hand to protect the families of the 27th Foot, which regiment had moved out to join the Mobile Column, in case the other native regiment in Nowshera—the 10th Irregular Cavalry—should show any signs of disaffection.

On the morning of the 24th Major Vaughan was informed that 800 bayonets of the 70th Foot, eight guns and a squadron of Multani Horse were then marching on Mardan for the purpose of disarming the 55th, said to be in a state of mutiny, and Major Vaughan was directed to co-operate by sending 200 rifles of his Regiment to join the Peshawar Column about Kurgh Deri, to the west of Mardan. Starting at 4 p.m. on the 24th, the rendezvous was reached shortly after daybreak next morning, but by this time the 55th, except about

* The officers with Major Vaughan were Lieutenants Williamson and Lind and Assistant Surgeon R. Rouse.

120 loyal men, had left Mardan and marched towards Swat, gaining so long a start that, though the pursuit was kept up for some miles by the infantry and further still by the Multani Horse, 120 men being killed and 140 made prisoners, the bulk of the mutineers escaped. At the end of the pursuit the 5th Punjab Infantry returned to Mardan, but was now attached to the Peshawar Column and sent for a time to the vicinity of Abazai, on the Swat River, to check the activities of a noted outlaw named Ajun Khan, who was suspected of intending to enter the Peshawar Valley and kindle a religious war. The Regiment underwent considerable hardships at this time owing to the absence of tents, and when early in June it returned to Mardan, Colonel Chute, commanding the Column, published the following :—

" *Colonel Chute, Commanding the Field Force, cannot permit the 5th Punjab Infantry to leave the force under his command without expressing his best thanks to Major Vaughan and the officers and men of his Regiment for their valuable services at Hoti Mardan on the 25th ult., and also for their excellent conduct while under his command in camp and quarters.*"

The Regiment now remained until the end of the year with Headquarters at Mardan, where its chief duty was to keep the peace on the Yusafzai border, a task heretofore carried out by the Corps of Guides. The country on and immediately beyond our border was at this time in an unusually disturbed state, due to the fact that the remnants of the 55th Native Infantry, carrying their arms, had sought refuge with the independent tribes ; while a recent revolution in Swat had excited the minds of the warlike and lately tamed people in Yusafzai, and caused them to intrigue against British rule. The result was that on at least three occasions during the next few months the Regiment was called upon to assist in operations against the neighbouring tribesmen.

On July 2nd Major Vaughan moved out with two guns, 80 sabres and 270 rifles of his own Regiment against certain Yusafzai villages on the Panjtar and Khodu Khel border, engaged and pursued the enemy and burnt the offending villages. Again, on July 18th, Major Vaughan marched out with four guns, a troop of cavalry, 300 rifles of the 4th and 400 of the 5th Punjab Infantry against the strong mountain village of

Narinji, which had become an asylum for certain firebrands known as the Hindustani fanatics and local bad characters. The village was attacked unsuccessfully, the enemy making a very gallant defence, frequently counter-attacking sword in hand. The retirement was unopposed, but the losses in Major Vaughan's force had not been inconsiderable, amounting to four men killed and twenty wounded, the majority of the losses falling upon the 5th Punjab Infantry, which had Sepoys Ghafur Khan and Shadah killed, and Jemadar Karam Khan, Bugler Sikandar and Sepoys Sawan, Phula Singh, Badawah Singh, Nathu, Jowaya, Sharfah, Jiwah, Bahadur Shah, Abdul Aziz, Fateh and Mozah Khan wounded.

Later it was decided that the village of Narinji should be re-attacked and totally destroyed, and, Major Vaughan's column having been very considerably reinforced, the operations were resumed on August 3rd and carried to a successful conclusion with but slight loss, only one man being killed and eight wounded, five of the latter belonging to the 5th Punjab Infantry.

The Regiment returned to Mardan on the conclusion of these operations, and now the four additional companies, ordered to be raised in May, were transferred to the 8th Punjab Infantry, while the original eight companies were now divided into ten.

Under authority of a letter from the Military Secretary to the Chief Commissioner, dated Lahore, August 17th, two handsome *lungis* were ordered to be presented to Subadar Lal Khan and Jemadar Aziz Khan in recognition of their gallant conduct in action at Narinji on August 3rd.

The 5th Punjab Infantry was now ordered to proceed to a larger field of action.

During the seven months which had elapsed since the outbreak of the Mutiny of the Bengal Army, very much had happened; the siege of Delhi had come to an end and Lucknow had been relieved, and the 5th Punjab Infantry was now ordered to march as rapidly as possible down country with a view to its joining the army with which Sir Colin Campbell was preparing for the recapture of Lucknow.

It was on January 3rd, 1858, that the Regiment commenced what was virtually a forced march towards Hindustan, the Commander-in-Chief's appreciation of the efforts made finding expression in letter

No. 255 from the D.A.Q.M.General to the Commanding Officer, dated Camp Cawnpore, February 4th :—

"*His Excellency the Commander-in-Chief desires me to convey to you his approval of the rapid progress you are making with your Regiment down country.*"

Before, however, this month came to an end, Sir Colin Campbell had already advanced with his army from Cawnpore for the final attack on Lucknow; and on the 14th, by which date the Regiment had arrived at Meerut on its downward march, it was there halted by order of Major-General Penny, commanding the Meerut Division, and was then attached to a force which, under command of that officer, marched towards Aligarh and Khasgunge. Consequently it was not until March 19th that Major Vaughan was ordered to march his Regiment to Lucknow, where it arrived on April 2nd. A week later the Headquarters and six companies were attached to a field force under Major-General Sir Hope Grant, K.C.B., to whom had been entrusted the task of hunting down the various dispersed bodies of armed men who were scattered over the province of Oude, whence the majority of the mutineers had come, and on April 11th this force marched towards Sitapore.

On April 13th Grant's troops expelled from the neighbourhood of Baree a considerable body of rebels under a noted leader, known as the Lucknow Maulvi, but the infantry of the force—the 38th Foot, the 2nd Battalion Rifle Brigade, the 1st Bengal Fusiliers and the 5th Punjab Infantry—was not seriously engaged, and the troops returned by a circuitous route to Lucknow, arriving there on the 27th. Next day the force marched through the Biswara district, and on May 13th attacked a large body of rebels in the jungle about Simri. Here, the left being threatened by the enemy, Nos. 9 and 10 Companies of the 5th Punjab Infantry first, and then the whole Regiment and Brigade, changed front and advanced, the front being covered by the above-named companies in skirmishing order. These came upon a large body of the enemy protected by a deep nullah, but they attacked in a most spirited manner and with complete success, killing many of the rebels and causing the hurried retreat of the remainder before their supports could come up.

No. 9—a comparatively newly raised company, composed wholly of Pathans—particularly distinguished itself on this occasion, and had one private killed, an Indian officer and seven privates wounded; these were Sepoy Sahib Alam killed; Jemadar Reman Khan, Sepoys Juma Khan, Mahammed Khan, Akbar, Abdul Mahammed, Ali Gul, Manah Singh and Jowahir Singh, wounded.

On June 13th Sir Hope Grant attacked a body of some 16,000 rebels who had taken up a strong position at Nawabgunge, sixteen miles from Lucknow, severely defeating them and capturing six guns. On this occasion the 5th Punjab Infantry came for the first time under artillery fire, and showed great steadiness and spirit when advancing against the guns.

Sir Hope Grant's column now spent a month or more at Nawabgunge in much discomfort owing to the heavy rain that fell; but on July 22nd he moved out with one troop Horse Artillery, a field battery, the 7th Hussars, 2nd Battalion Rifle Brigade, Madras Fusiliers and 5th Punjab Infantry in the direction of Fyzabad, with the object of assisting a local Raja who had signified his allegiance to the Company and was besieged by the rebels in his fort at Shahgunge. The approach of the force was sufficient to cause the dispersal of the Raja's opponents, and Sir Hope Grant then moved upon and occupied Fyzabad.

Here the force was reorganized, and the 5th Punjab Infantry, with a troop of Horse Artillery, the 7th Hussars, the Madras Fusiliers and some Madras Sappers, was placed under the command of Brigadier-General Horsford and ordered to march on Sultanpore, where the rebels were said to be assembling in some strength. By reason of the rainy season the roads were very heavy, and the heat being very great, the men suffered a good deal.

Brigadier-General Horsford arrived near Sultanpore on the left bank of the Gumti on the 11th, when the 5th was sent forward with two guns to reconnoitre the enemy's position and occupy the town, and it was found that a large body of the rebels had crossed to the left bank. They were immediately attacked and driven across the Gumti, from the further bank of which they opened a heavy gun and rifle fire upon No. 1 Company of the Regiment, then lining the left bank; their fire was, however, met and overcome by that of our guns and of the other companies of the Regiment as these came up in support.

General Horsford was unable to cross the river, as he had no bridging material with him and the rebels had removed or destroyed all the boats ; so that, pending the arrival of bridge material and reinforcements, this small force had to picquet some six miles of river bank to keep the enemy in check, a duty which was very harassing, but which afforded the 5th Punjab Infantry a very valuable experience.

On the 22nd General Grant came up from Fyzabad with reinforcements, rafts were constructed and arrangements made for transporting the force to the right bank of the river. By the morning of the 24th all was in readiness, and the crossing of the Gumti has been described as follows by two officers then serving with the force. One writes* :—
" There were no losses from the enemy's fire in crossing. The heavy battery had opened as soon as it was light enough, and had swept the enemy from the opposite bank, so the crossing was unopposed. . . . The Madras European Fusiliers and the Punjab Battalion having gone over on a raft, formed rapidly in column of companies for the advance, and were not kept long waiting by the gunners. Twenty minutes after the last horse had scrambled up the bank with his Sikh rider hanging on to his tail, the teams were harnessed and the guns advanced into action at the steady trot peculiar to field batteries."

The other writer† states :—" Grant, after some delay, had got his troops across the river and was about to attack the rebel force opposed to us. My regiment was skirmishing to the front to cover the crossing when, looking to the rear, I saw that renowned old regiment, the 1st Madras Fusiliers, advancing towards us in line with its Colours flying and band playing. The effect was heightened by a grand sunset just behind the regiment, and the sight altogether was most soul-stirring. I need hardly say how heartily the 5th joined in the advance and how quickly the enemy judged discretion to be the better part of valour."

On August 29th the force advanced to and occupied the cantonment of Sultanpore, where the Headquarters of the Regiment remained for some six weeks, but detachments during this time joined other

* Bland Strange, " Gunner Jingo's Jubilee," p. 239.

† Vaughan, " My Service in the Indian Army and After," p. 82.

small columns operating in different parts of the province. Thus Nos. 4 and 5 Companies, under Captain W. D. Hoste, joined a small force which was sent to take up a position at Burtipore and Sailkah on the Fyzabad road, and while thus detached Havildar Muza Khan, Naik Baz Gul and Sepoys Fazul Khan and Madi were specially brought to notice for gallant conduct and received promotion. Then on October 6th Nos. 6, 7 and 8 Companies, under Lieutenant and Adjutant C. E. Stewart, were attached to another column which marched to beat up some rebel bodies to the eastward about the Azimgarh border. Finally, on the 10th of the same month the Headquarters of the 5th Punjab Infantry marched with a large force, under General Grant's personal command, to expel the rebels from the eastern portion of Oude before advancing against the forts of Amethee and Sunkurpore.

The Regiment was finally united at Sultanpore on October 24th, and during the remainder of the year was engaged as a whole, or in detachments of varying size, under the Commander-in-Chief himself or under Colonels Galwey and Christie, in the operations in the valleys of the Gumti and Gogra rivers, having for their object the clearing of the few remaining rebel bands from Oude and of driving them into Nepal territory beyond the River Raptee. By the end of the year these objects had been achieved and the bulk of the Commander-in-Chief's army was broken up; but a considerable force of all arms, in which the 5th was included, remained at Sidonia Ghat on the Raptee to prevent the rebels from working back into Oude.

The operations which now ensued were carried out in very difficult country and involved the Regiment in no fewer than three incursions across the Nepal border; and even when General Horsford's column was broken up in March, the 5th Punjab Infantry remained on service in this part of the country until the end of the year 1859, constantly engaged in fighting with large and small parties of the rebels. For their services the following were favourably mentioned in despatches :—Major J. L. Vaughan, Captain W. D. Hoste, Lieutenants S. J. Browne and W. J. Forlong, Subadars Aziz Khan, Nihal Singh and Habib Khan, Havildar Musa Khan, Naik Habibullah Khan and Sepoy Fakir Shah, the two last-named being awarded the 3rd Class of the Order of Merit for killing Bakht Khan, once a Subadar of the Bengal Army, the prime mover in the mutiny of the Bareilly Brigade, and lately a general in the rebel army during the siege of Delhi.

The Regimental Digest records that during the operations in Oude the 5th Punjab Infantry had four men killed and eleven wounded.

In Field Orders of December 26th by Brigadier Holdich, C.B., Commanding the Trans-Gogra and Gorakhpore districts, in which the Regiment was serving, the 5th Punjab Infantry was ordered, on relief by a detachment of the Moradabad Levy, to march from Bahraich to Cawnpore *en route* to Lahore with a view to its return to the Frontier. In the same Order the Brigadier bade farewell to the Regiment in the following laudatory terms :—

"*On the departure of the 5th Punjab Rifles from the Oude frontier district, the Brigadier would record his appreciation of the services rendered by Lieut.-Colonel Vaughan and the Regiment under his command.*"

The operations connected with the suppression of the Mutiny having come to an end, the Indian authorities had now to prepare a force to accompany the allied armies to China, and in G.G.O. No. 52, dated December 20th, 1859, certain corps of cavalry and infantry were asked whether they were inclined to volunteer for this new service. On December 29th Lieut.-Colonel Vaughan informed the Secretary to the Government of India, Military Department, that on that day there were 678 men of all ranks at Headquarters, and that of this number 475 volunteered for service in China and that 203 did not ; later, however, some of the volunteers appear to have changed their minds, and the final figures obtained on January 14th, 1860, showed that 385 expressed their readiness to go to China and 292 refused, the Sikhs evincing a much greater willingness to volunteer than did the Pathans, Punjabi Mahammedans and Dogras of the Regiment.

It should be remembered that the men had now been in the field for two and a half years and had had no regular cantonment for nearly three ; while they felt with much justice that they had honourably completed the service for which they had been brought down from the Punjab.

In General Vaughan's reminiscences it is stated that "On the representation of Sir John Lawrence that the regiments of the Frontier Force had only been lent for the suppression of the Mutiny, and should now revert to their proper duty, the defence of the trans-Indus frontier, the destination of my Regiment was changed, and it was ordered to return to Kohat." There is, however, no mention of this in any of the "Lives" of Lord Lawrence, who, moreover, had left India in February, 1859—ten months before the appearance of the G.G.O. above referred to—and did not return until 1864!

Marching back to the Punjab, the 5th Infantry arrived at Kohat on April 11th, 1860, and after remaining there nearly a year was ordered to Dera Ismail Khan, where, during the next six months, it was employed, in conjunction with the 6th Punjab Infantry, in assisting in the blockade of the Mahsud Waziris, supplying strong garrisons for the defence of the frontier posts.

In this year the establishment was reduced from ten to eight companies and the office of Native Adjutant was abolished, the grade of Subadar-Major being introduced in its place. Nos. 6 and 7 Companies were broken up, and the Regiment was now composed of three companies of Sikhs, three of Pathans, and one each of Punjabi Mahammedans and Dogras.

Two very important matters must now be mentioned, the one inaugurating a very great change in the government of British India, the other concerned with the reorganization of the Indian Army. Early in 1858 Lord Palmerston brought in a Bill "for the better government of British India," the avowed object of which was the transfer of the authority of the East India Company to the Crown. The passage of the Bill into law was delayed by the overthrow of Lord Palmerston's Government, but his successor introduced a similar measure which became law in August, 1858, and was made known in India on November 1st by a Royal Proclamation. The clause affecting the Indian Army stated that the military Services of the Company should be deemed to be those of Her Majesty, and to be under the same obligations to serve the Queen as they had been to serve the Company, while continuing to enjoy all their former emoluments and privileges.

The year 1860 saw the introduction of the Staff Corps. "This was the outcome of the disappearance during the Mutiny of nearly the whole of the Regular regiments of the Bengal Army, and their replacement by Irregular regiments. But as under the Irregular system the number of British officers with each corps was too limited to admit of their promotion being carried on regimentally, as had been done under the Regular system, some organization had to be devised by which the pay and promotion of all officers joining the Indian Army in future could be arranged. Many schemes were put forward ; eventually one formulated by Colonel Norman was, with certain modifications, accepted by the Secretary of State, the result being that all officers about to enter the Indian Army were to be placed on one list, in which they would be promoted after fixed periods of service ; and all those officers who had been thrown out of employment by the disbandment of their regiments or by the substitution of the Irregular for the Regular system were to have the option of joining it."*

On January 3rd, 1863, the Regiment, then at Kohat, received the medals granted for service in the Indian Mutiny Campaign. This was the first Royal Medal awarded to the Indian Army.

On October 7th, 1863, the 5th Punjab Infantry marched to join the Yusafzai Field Force, formed for service against the Hindustani fanatics of Malka who had lately occupied Sittana without any objection being raised by the neighbouring tribes, although they, at the close of the 1858 expedition against these fanatics, had assured the Indian Government that they would not permit these people to settle in or near their territories. The Hindustanis now commenced raiding into Hazara, carrying off rich Hindus for ransom, while the Maulvi Abdulla and other firebrands began preaching *jihad.* An expedition on a large scale was now sanctioned for the punishment of these people, and the force employed was to be under the command of Brigadier-General N. Chamberlain.

The troops detailed for the expedition were to be divided into two columns, the one operating from the Peshawar Valley, the other from Hazara, the former assembling at Nawa Killa and Swabi, moving through the Ambeyla Pass and thence by Koga in the Chamla Valley and Chirori on Sittana ; the Hazara column was to remain at Darband to overawe the riverain tribes and protect the Hazara border, while other troops were to hold the line of the Indus and certain posts on the Hazara and Yusafzai borders. Hostility was not anticipated from the

* Lord Roberts, "Forty-one Years in India," Vol. I, pp. 485-6.

people of Buner, who had no quarrel with the Indian Government, and no religious or other sympathy with the Hindustani fanatics; but, unfortunately, it was impossible to give notice to the Bunerwals that their country was to be approached and the Ambeyla Pass made use of, and consequently they imagined that the invasion and possible annexation of their country was intended, and in the end they also took up arms against us.

By the morning of October 19th the bulk of the force was concentrated at Nawa Killa, and on the evening of the same day the 5th Punjab Infantry moved forward with the advance column under Colonel Wilde, C.B., and by early the next morning had reached, with but slight opposition, the crest of the Ambeyla Pass, and, moving on down the pass, camp was pitched on the further slopes. It was very soon clear that the Bunerwals had thrown in their lot with the rest of the tribesmen, and it was equally evident that the settlements of the Hindustani fanatics on the Mahabun Mountain could not be reached by the Chamla Valley with a strong enemy force on the left flank; so the force under General Chamberlain settled down to strengthen its position and improve the communications with the rear, the General hoping that the effect of unsuccessful attacks upon him would discourage the enemy and cause the break-up of the coalition.

On the night of the 22nd an attack was made upon the upper left picquets of the camp, and the 5th Punjab Infantry was called up to reinforce these, and assisted in repelling the enemy. From now onwards the Regiment was permanently attached to these defences, and took a prominent part in the severe action fought here on the 26th. No. 4 Company, under Lieutenant S. Beckett, behaved with remarkable steadiness in supporting and covering the retirement of the 6th Punjab Infantry. Of the services of the Regiment this day Brigadier Chamberlain reported as follows:—

"*The 5th Punjab Infantry, under Lieutenant Stewart, had been chiefly employed to cover and support the guns, one company of which regiment, under Lieutenant Beckett, did excellent service in supporting the advance of the 6th Punjab Infantry, and it withdrew in the best order after the 6th Punjab Infantry regained its position.*"

On October 29th the Regiment was detailed to find the garrison for the very exposed and important post known as the " Eagle's Nest," where the defenders were under a close and persistent fire from the enemy marksmen on the Guru Mountain ; here the Regiment remained until November 18th, when this and other picquets on the Guru were withdrawn, the retirement being covered by Lieutenant Beckett, Subadar Aziz Khan and part of No. 4 Company. During the fighting of the same day another company was sent under Lieutenant E. S. Fox as a reinforcement to a picquet which was hard pressed and did excellent service.

For a day or two now the men of the 5th were employed in constructing and holding a new post called the " Water Picquet " ; but on the 20th about 220 men—all that could be spared from the defences of the Upper Camp—assisted in the recovery of the " Crag Picquet," which had been for the third time captured by the enemy. Brigadier Chamberlain stated in his despatch that—

" *Lieutenant Beckett was one of the first to reach the summit, and also foremost in entering the work on the left.*"

On this day Lieut.-Colonel Vaughan, commanding a column, was wounded.

During the month of December a portion of the force moved out against the enemy, but the 5th remained behind, Lieut.-Colonel Vaughan being placed in charge of the camp. During the afternoon of the 15th the enemy made an attack, when an opportunity of doing very gallant service was afforded No. 8 Company, under Lieutenant Fox ; the company had been sent to reinforce what was known as the " Advanced Picquet," and joined in a very gallant charge made by the rest of the picquet upon the enemy.

By this time the objects of the expedition were considered to have been achieved, the Bunerwals showed a disposition to make peace and even to destroy Malka and expel the Hindustani fanatics ; while the tribesmen who had taken the field against us had suffered serious loss. On December 23rd, then, the force was broken up and the 5th Punjab Infantry was ordered to return to Kohat.

During the campaign the Regiment had been almost throughout commanded by Lieutenant C. E. Stewart, Lieut.-Colonel Vaughan having usually exercised a higher command. The losses sustained were—

Killed, Havildar Syadiwali, Naik Rukken-ud-Din, Sepoys Suku, Bahawal Khan, Habib, Juma Khan, Mahammed Din and Fattah; wounded, Lieut.-Colonel J. L. Vaughan, Jemadars Elahi Bakhsh and Rahman Khan, Naik Kadir Bakhsh, Sepoys Zerib Khan, Syad Mahammed, Nek Mahammed, Fakir Khan, Pir Bakhsh, Hyat, Ramzan, Jamal Din, Fattah Khan, Suchetah, Niaz Gul, Fakir, Mirzoki, Nek Mahammed II, and Langri Gurmukh Singh.

To officers and other ranks of the Regiment the following decorations were awarded:—To Lieut.-Colonel J. L. Vaughan, the C.B.; to Subadar Aziz Khan and Jemadar Rahman Khan, the 2nd Class, and to Havildar Sher Gul the 3rd Class of the Order of Merit—the two last for endeavouring to save the life of a British soldier at the "Crag Picquet" on November 20th.

For nearly ten years after the close of the Ambeyla Campaign the Regiment was not called upon for the performance of other than the routine duties of one of the Frontier Corps; during 1864 and 1865 it remained at Kohat, and in 1865 was the best shooting regiment of all the infantry of the Punjab Irregular Force. In the early hot weather of 1866 the 5th marched to Bannu, when, after the inspection in February, 1867, Brigadier-General Wilde, C.B., Commanding the Force, reported on the Regiment in the following terms:—

"*The Regiment looked as well as formerly and the men are a fine, soldier-like body, steady, clean and well dressed. While the Regiment is one of the best Light Infantry Corps in the Punjab Frontier Force,* * *it is one of the most silent and steady under arms.*"

In January, 1869, the 5th marched in relief to Dera Ismail Khan, and in the February of the year following to Jatta, where for some six weeks it was employed in covering the workmen who were sinking a well near the Girni Pass, preparatory to a post being established there. The distance from the camp to the Pass was upwards of seven miles over broken and very stony ground; and, as the men employed had to go and return on the same day, this entailed a march of fourteen miles, the men having to be under arms and on the alert the whole time, for the spot was close under the Waziri hills and much exposed to attack.

* The new designation was adopted under authority of Mil. Dept. letter No. 279 of September 19th, 1865.

This duty completed in March, 1870, the Regiment formed part of a force under Lieut.-Colonel T. G. Kennedy which on the 17th marched to Kot Khirgi, in the low hills on the Waziri border, and was there employed in protecting the building of a larger post, and on May 8th started to march back to Dera Ismail Khan. For their services at Girni and Kot Khirgi officers and men received the thanks of Government, Major F. H. Jenkins and Subadar Rahman Khan being particularly mentioned in Colonel Kennedy's report.

In April, 1871, the whole Regiment was re-armed with the Enfield rifle, the old two-grooved Brunswick rifle being returned to the arsenal.

On October 10th, 1871, the Indian General Service Medals granted under the terms of G.G.O. No. 812 of 1869 were received at the Headquarters of the Regiment and distributed to all entitled to receive them. Up to this time officers and other ranks of the Punjab Frontier Force had received no medals for any of the expeditions on and beyond the North-West Frontier in which they had taken part; but by the General Order above quoted the India Medal, with clasp "North West Frontier," was now granted to the survivors of the troops which had been engaged in some thirteen expeditions from 1849-1860, and by the same G.G.O. a clasp was also granted for "Ambeyla" or, as spelt on the clasp, "Umbeyla."

In this month the Regiment was again sent to Girni to cover the erection of a post, make a road from Girni to Kot Khirgi, and to erect a tower at the mouth of the Girni Pass, receiving the thanks of the Supreme and Punjab Governments for the good service rendered; from here it marched to the mouth of the Tank Zam Pass to protect the building of the Zam Post, and then, on relief by the 6th Punjab Infantry, marched to quarters at Dera Ghazi Khan, where it arrived on March 7th, 1872.

On October 10th two companies, under Captain C. E. Stewart, marched to Lahore and formed part of the escort of the Lieutenant-Governor of the Punjab during his winter tour of inspection along the frontier, rejoining Headquarters on May 3rd, 1873, having been for seven months on the march or in camp.

At the end of 1874 the 5th Punjab Infantry was ordered to Abbottabad, and during its stay here suffered very severely from pneumonia, losing by death 1 Indian officer, 3 non-commissioned officers, 15 privates, 5 buglers and 9 camp followers.

In December the Regiment received a sufficient number of Snider rifles to re-arm four companies, and by January 19th of the year following the whole Regiment was thus armed.

In consequence of the menacing attitude taken up this summer by the tribes of the Black Mountain, and the probability of an attack by them on the Agror Valley, the Regiment was called upon at a moment's notice on June 23rd to send a reinforcement of one British officer and 106 other ranks to the post at Oghi, forty miles from Abbottabad. Within less than three hours of receipt of orders the detachment was on the march, and covered the distance, in great heat, in thirteen and a half hours. Of this performance the Commandant of the Punjab Frontier Force wrote as follows on July 3rd :—

" *The alacrity displayed by the detachment 5th Punjab Infantry in marching to Oghi at three hours' notice in less than fourteen hours on the night of June 23rd is very creditable both to officers and men.*"

During the ensuing cold weather certain regiments of the Punjab Frontier Force, the 5th among them, were ordered to join the camp of exercise at Delhi, which was attended by H.R.H. the Prince of Wales (King Edward VII), returning to Abbottabad on March 10th, 1876, after an absence of five months. During the camp the Regiment formed part of the 2nd Brigade, 4th Division, and won golden opinions from those under whom it served. On its return to the Punjab, Brigadier-General C. P. Keyes, C.B., Commanding the Punjab Frontier Force, published in orders the following remarks from Major-General Stewart and Brigadier-General Ross, prefacing these by the following words from himself :—

" *The state of discipline and general efficiency of the Corps, which elicited such high praise from such distinguished officers, is highly creditable to Major McQueen and the Regiment generally.*"

From Major-General Stewart, C.B., Commanding 4th Division :—

" *It is due to Major McQueen, Commanding the 5th Punjab Infantry, that I should place on record the opinion I formed of his Regiment during the time it served under my command at the Camp of Exercise lately assembled at Delhi.*

"*In all executive points I found the Regiment to be in excellent order, and I do not hesitate to say that it is fit for any service. The men composing the Corps are a remarkably fine body, and I was particularly struck by their zealous and soldier-like bearing, and the cheerfulness with which they did their work under circumstances which often exposed them to a good deal of discomfort and much real fatigue. The condition of the Regiment is most creditable to Major McQueen and his officers, and I should esteem it a favour if you will cause the substance of this letter to be communicated to the Regiment.*"

From Brigadier-General Ross, Commanding 2nd Infantry Brigade, 4th Division :—

"*During the period at the Camp of Exercise, Delhi,* 1875-76, *that the 5th Punjab Infantry formed a portion of the Brigade under my command, I formed the highest opinion of Major McQueen as commanding officer and of the Regiment generally.*

"*I consider the officers, European and Native, smart and well-instructed, and the men a fine and efficient body of soldiers.*"

In 1877 Sepoy Narain Singh, "F" Company, won the Magdala Gold Medal for shooting.

The 5th Punjab Infantry was called upon in this year to take part in certain operations which were sanctioned by Government, against a branch of the Adam Khel Afridis inhabiting the hilly country between the districts of Peshawar and Kohat. During the days when the Sikhs ruled at Peshawar, the Adam Khel had received an allowance for keeping open the Peshawar—Kohat road, by which these two towns are no more than 37 miles apart, only ten miles being in independent territory, while round by way of Khushalgarh on the Indus the distance is some 200 miles. This allowance the Indian Government had continued, but there was now some idea of reducing the allowance given to the Jawaki branch of the Adam Khel, who in recent troubles had shown themselves unable or unwilling to carry out the service expected of them and for which they were paid. The Jawakis live to the east of the Kohat Pass, inhabiting the valleys forming the southern portion of the Adam Khel country and also the northern Bori Valley, and were thus well placed to give trouble. In July they began to show signs of hostility, cutting the telegraph wire in several places and their *jirgas* refusing to come in when called upon to answer for these outrages.

On October 10th a Wing and the Headquarters of the Regiment marched with a wing of the 5th Gurkhas to Shadipore on the Indus to assist in protecting that part of the Kohat border from raids by the Jawakis; and while encamped at Lukka Talao, three miles from the border, one of the Regimental picquets under Jemadar Sham Singh was attacked by the tribesmen, who, however, very quickly retreated on the Khattak company moving up in support.

Next morning the column, now under Major McQueen, moved out to reconnoitre the Numdari Pass—a very rugged, narrow defile with commanding heights on the north. The crest was seized without opposition, and a Jawaki picquet of upwards of twenty men narrowly escaped capture. The retirement on camp, covered by two companies of the 5th, was followed up, but the enemy avoided coming to close quarters and no casualties were incurred.

While at Lukka Talao the Paia and Gaoz-Darrah valleys and the Nanung Pass were all reconnoitred, and the villages of Shadipore, Pushtu Chunda and Saim were put in a state of defence, the ground all round being cleared of jungle. The work was hard, but nothing could exceed the spirit and energy with which the men worked.

Early in November precise orders for the conduct of punitive operations to be carried out against the Jawakis were issued to Brigadier-General C. P. Keyes, and a force wholly composed of Punjab troops was organized in three columns, 280 rifles of the 5th Punjab Infantry being in No. 3 Column under Colonel Gardiner of the 5th Gurkhas. An advance was made on November 9th, and while Columns 1 and 2, advancing respectively by the Tortang and Gandiali Passes, rendezvoused at Turki and thence occupied the Paia valley, No. 3 Column moved forward by way of the Nanung Pass on the village of Kahkto.

Lieutenant Mein, with a company of the Regiment, formed the advanced guard, until the enemy was met with on the heights at the crest of the Pass; these opening a heavy fire, a second company was sent forward under Lieutenant G. Gaisford, and the two combining, drove the enemy from ridge to ridge in a very dashing manner.

The country through which the column—its advance covered by

the 5th Punjab Infantry—now had to move, consisted of a very dense thorn jungle, intersected by large ravines, with here and there low ridges, the valley now entered upon being about a mile and a half wide, enclosed by high hills. There was no serious opposition until the column had advanced some three miles from the Nanung Pass, when it was found that the Jawakis had taken up a strong position on a ridge with a deep ravine in front; but the men of the Regiment, rapidly closing with the enemy, charged up the hill and drove him off, inflicting severe punishment, ten of the tribesmen being here killed and many wounded. There was no further opposition, and No. 3 Column now joined the rest of Brigadier-General Keyes' force in the Paia valley.

On November 12th a company of the Regiment under Major C. E. Stewart, which had been sent up the Tumbal Pitao range to the south, in order to drive off some of the enemy who were annoying the foraging parties, was suddenly attacked in very broken and precipitous ground by superior numbers who entirely outflanked them. The company first drove the enemy back, taking up a good position, but towards evening, when it was time to fall back on the camp, the enemy followed up and charged, sword in hand. The men of the 5th, gallantly led by Major Stewart and Lieutenant Gaisford, met the enemy with a counter-charge, killed two and wounded others, regaining the position they had just left. The enemy was by this so thoroughly disheartened that he at once drew off. Three of the company—Sepoys Abdul Ghafur, Muktiara and Hari Singh—were wounded, while Lieutenant Gaisford was specially mentioned by Major Stewart for his gallant and dashing conduct. Six men—Sepoys Abdul Ghafur, Said Shah, Lal Khan, Bassawah Singh, Urjun and Phaugan—were recommended for the Order of Merit, which was eventually awarded to the three first named.

The force now left the Paia valley and took up a position in the Turki valley, preparatory to an advance on Jamu, one of the main strongholds in the Jawaki country; but heavy rain delayed operations for some days, during which Sepoy Dassu of the Regiment was killed during one of the many attacks made on the picquets.

On December 1st the Regiment was well in the advance of the right column of attack on Jamu, and again on the 7th when the village of Ghariba was captured; on neither occasion was there any serious opposition, nor was the force very actively followed up on retirement. In the attack on Ghariba, Lieutenant J. E. Mein and Subadar-Major Aziz Khan led the skirmishers of the Corps.

After the capture of Ghariba, General Keyes' force was withdrawn to the camp in front of Bagh, and it was not until December 31st that a combined advance on Pustawani, in conjunction with another column from Peshawar, could be commenced. On this day the Regiment formed part of the advance column which was to ascend the Durgai heights and enable the main body to move up the mountain path leading to Walai. This was carried out unopposed, and the 5th bivouacked that night on the Durgai heights. On the following day, when the whole force retired from the very high and precipitous mountain, the Regiment was detailed to cover the movement, and Lieutenant Gaisford, with "B" and "D" Companies under Subadar-Major Aziz Khan, were chiefly concerned in this very difficult and onerous duty. The enemy, who had mustered in force, and whose knowledge of the ground gave him a great advantage, attacked heavily; but these officers withdrew their men so skilfully that there were no casualties, while the men, in this most difficult of all retirements, conspicuously displayed the most perfect coolness and discipline, holding their ground against overwhelming numbers till ordered to retire.

That evening the Regiment returned to camp at Shindeh with the rest of the force.

For some weeks longer the 5th Punjab Infantry remained in the Jawaki country, furnishing escorts to survey and exploring parties; but by the beginning of March, 1878, the Jawakis having submitted, paid a fine and given hostages for future good behaviour, the force was broken up, and on March 7th the Headquarter Wing marched into Kohat, where a month later it was joined by the Left Wing from Abbottabad under Captain C. M. Hall.

Of the services of the regiments under his command General Keyes wrote :—

"*I now desire to bring to the notice of Government the admirable conduct of the troops throughout these operations. At Paia the men not actually on duty had tolerably fair shelter, but immediately after we had taken up new positions at Shindeh and Turki they were exposed to thirty-six hours' rain with scarcely any shelter, and again not many days afterwards seventy hours' almost continuous rain under similar circumstances. They were without any change of clothes for nearly a month; night duty was exceptionally heavy in consequence of the extended nature of our position, yet the spirits of our men never flagged, their cheerfulness and endurance under the hardships occasioned by the unseasonable and unusually heavy rain were beyond all praise.*"

Since April, 1876, when Lord Lytton had assumed the office of Viceroy, Russia had seriously extended her empire in an easterly direction. The Russian Governor of Turkestan had made frequent overtures to Sher Ali, the Amir of Afghanistan, whose attitude towards the Indian Government had been unfriendly if not yet actually hostile; and while he refused to receive a mission which Lord Lytton proposed to send to Kabul, intelligence reached India that the Amir had admitted to and favourably received in his country a mission sent thither from Russia. It seemed necessary for the maintenance of our prestige to insist upon the reception on equal terms of a British envoy, to the office of which General Chamberlain was appointed; but on his proceeding in September, 1878, to the Khyber Pass *en route* to Kabul, accompanied by a small escort, he was turned back at Ali Musjid by the Amir's local representative.

On November 2nd something of the nature of an ultimatum was forwarded to the Amir, demanding an apology and the acceptance of a permanent British mission at Kabul; and no reply to these demands having been received within the period of grace allowed, war was declared against the Amir, Sher Ali Khan, on the 21st of that month.

Four columns were detailed for the advance into Afghanistan, and the 5th Punjab Infantry was told off to the 1st Brigade of the Kurram Valley Column, under Major-General F. S. Roberts, V.C., C.B., the Brigade being commanded by Brigadier-General A. H. Cobbe, while also included in it were the 2nd Bn. 8th Foot, the 23rd Pioneers and the 29th Bengal Native Infantry.

On October 8th the Regiment marched to Thal, where it arrived on the 13th, and was here employed until the day of the advance in making roads; but at this date the 5th could only muster 325 men, owing to the sickness which had lately prevailed and to the fact that

GENERAL SIR J. W. McQUEEN, G.C.B.

many men were on furlough. Recruiting parties had, however, been sent out, and every effort was being made to recruit the Regiment up to a strength of 800 privates.

The Kurram Valley Field Force crossed the Kurram River on November 21st and advanced up the valley, arriving at Kurram Fort, fifty-two miles from Thal, without meeting any opposition. On the 28th the Regiment formed part of the advanced guard, which was commanded by Major McQueen, in the forward move on the Peiwar Kotal; here the Afghans were found in position on very strong ground, and they used their artillery to such effect that the attacking party was unable to turn the position. Consequently, as evening was coming on, the advanced troops were withdrawn, the 5th Punjab Infantry, as the official account states, "covering the movement admirably," and the column halted for three or four days to enable supplies to come up. The retirement was conducted by Major H. M. Pratt with great judgment and skill, and he was ably seconded by Captain C. M. Hall, Lieutenant R. F. Jameson and the Indian officers in command of companies.

In this affair of the 28th the following men were wounded:—Subadar-Major Aziz Khan, Bahadur, very severely; Sepoys Kaim Khan, Ghulam Mahammed, Jowahir Singh and Miah Singh. Subadar-Major Aziz Khan, Bahadur, died on January 5th, 1879, from the effects of this wound, and in him the Regiment lost one of the finest and bravest Indian officers in the Service, and the Government a distinguished and loyal servant. The following Regimental Order, No. 201 A, of January 6th, bears testimony to the esteem in which he was held, and is a record of his distinguished services:—

"*It is with deep regret that the Commanding Officer has to announce the death at Kurram Fort on the 5th inst. of Subadar-Major Aziz Khan, Bahadur, from the effects of a severe gun-shot wound received at Peiwar on November 28th, 1878, and he desires to place on record the very brilliant services of that gallant soldier, and at the same time to acknowledge how much he was always personally indebted to Subadar-Major Aziz Khan for his ready help, advice and great tact in the management of the men.*

"*All ranks in the Regiment must feel their great loss in a leader of such experience and cool and dashing courage, and one whose name was proverbial amongst them for liberality and kindness, and whose very distinguished conduct and services afford such a brilliant example to all.*

"*Twice was Subadar-Major Aziz Khan decorated with the Order of Merit for distinguished gallantry in the field. He was also awarded the Order of British India for long, good and faithful service, as well as being given a Turban of Honour by Sir John Lawrence in* 1857, *and later on a Dress and Sword of Honour by Sir Henry Davies, Lieutenant-Governor of the Punjab.*"

When, on December 1st, a second attempt to carry the Peiwar Kotal was made by the bulk of the column, the enemy fell back to a position in rear which they defended with much determination, and for some time no advantage was gained by either side. At last the 5th Punjab Infantry, which had been left behind in camp, ascended a long and thickly-wooded spur in front of the enemy's left centre, and was able to bring a heavy and effective fire on some of the Afghan guns and infantry. Later in the day Major McQueen was placed in charge of a second turning movement, having under his orders the 5th Gurkhas, the 5th Punjab Infantry and No. 1 Mountain Battery, and without a shot being fired, his advance, followed by that of the main body, was completely successful and the enemy evacuated his very strong position, leaving behind him 18 guns and large supplies of ammunition and grain.

In this action the Regiment had four men wounded—Sepoys Jung Khan, Taru, Karrak Singh and Asuf Khan.

On December 24th the Regiment started back to Kohat, escorting the captured guns, sick, wounded and prisoners, leaving again to join the Kurram Field Force on March 6th, 1879, escorting ten lakhs of treasure. Habib Killa was reached on the 23rd, and here the Corps occupied part of the old Afghan cantonment, afterwards joining the main body of the force, which by April 13th was concentrated on a plateau four miles east of Ali Khel. It remained here or in this neighbourhood until, on May 26th, a treaty of peace was signed at Gandamak with the new Amir, Yakub Khan. The bulk of the forces which had been employed did not, however, return to their stations on the North-West Frontier or in India, but remained temporarily where the end of this, the first phase of the campaign, had left them; and from the middle of June until early in September the 5th Punjab Infantry was in camp near Shalozan, midway between Kurram and the Peiwar Kotal. Here the Regiment was employed in road-making and in protecting the workmen engaged in laying out and building a fort and cantonment. There was an outbreak of cholera while here, the 5th having six cases, only one of which, however, proved fatal. It did, however, suffer some loss in an attack, made on July 29th upon a party of sixty-four men of all ranks proceeding on furlough, by a band of some 800 tribesmen on the Thal—Kohat road. The party was suddenly fired into from an ambush in the jungle and then charged by the Pathans sword in hand. The men of the Regiment, taken by surprise, had no time to load, but repulsed the enemy with the bayonet, the Indian officer in command, Subadar-Mirza Khan, and all his men behaving splendidly. The Subadar was wounded and died some months later from his wounds, and of his party three men were killed and seven wounded.

Late at night on September 4th news of the attack on the Kabul Residency reached the Political Officer at Ali Khel and was telegraphed to Simla. Later, details of the full extent of the tragedy were received, and at a meeting of the Council of India it was decided that a division under General Roberts should at once advance on Kabul; that another division should occupy Jalalabad; and that Kandahar be re-occupied and Ghazni threatened.

Some 6,000 men were collected at Ali Khel under General Roberts by September 12th, and the 5th Punjab Infantry marched on the morning of the 16th for the same place, being at once pushed forward from there to the Shutargarden. Before the main body of the Regiment arrived there, an advanced party under Lieutenant McKinstry, which was holding the Sirkai Kotal and Karatiga posts in the Hazar Darakht defile, was attacked on the 22nd, and had one man killed in driving off the Afghans. On the same day eight men of the Regiment in charge of Government stores, etc., between these posts, were suddenly overwhelmed, seven out of the eight being killed. The casualties in these two affairs were Lance-Naik Prem Singh, Sepoys Bur Singh, Habib, Jumal Khan, Balu, Kalu, Gulab Singh and Ramzan.

The Shutargarden was reached on the 23rd and Khushi on the 26th, 200 rifles having remained behind on the Sirkai Kotal under Captain Hall. While the force was moving up to and concentrating at Khushi, the Amir, Yakub Khan, arrived in camp and surrendered. The 5th Punjab Infantry was now in the 2nd Brigade under Brigadier-General T. D. Baker, with the 72nd Highlanders, 3rd Sikhs, 23rd Pioneers and 5th Gurkhas, and though General Roberts' force was able to commence its march towards Kabul on October 1st, carriage was so scarce and so indifferent that movement was slow and by portions only of the force at a time ; so that it was October 5th before the whole column arrived near Charasia, eleven miles from Kabul.

Next morning a wing of the Regiment under Captain Hall, later reinforced by 100 rifles under Lieutenant Sparling, took part in the attack by the 4,000 men now under General Roberts' immediate command, on the enemy position extending from the Sang-i-Nawishta Gorge to the hills north-west of Charasia. At the critical moment when the Afghan centre had to be assaulted, Captain Hall was directed to capture the key of the position ; this he did, "A" Company under Subadar Budh Singh leading the attack, driving the enemy from the breastworks and inflicting considerable loss upon him. For his gallantry on this occasion the Subadar was subsequently awarded the Order of Merit.

The casualties sustained by the Regiment in this affair were—killed : Jemadar Khani Mulla, Sepoys Labh Singh and Ditta and Bugler Jai Ram ; and wounded : Captain C. Young, Sepoys Chuttar Singh, Guran Ditla (died of wounds), Sundar and Jowalla Singh.

The Regiment occupied Kabul with the remainder of the division, and during the weeks that immediately followed was sent to the Shutargarden, marching down the Logar Valley on its return to the capital. Later it provided a detachment of 100 rifles to hold Butkak, and it also formed part of a force which visited Upper Maidan.

Early in December it became apparent that three enemy bodies were advancing on Kabul—from the south, from Kohistan and from Ghazni—and on the 9th General Roberts sent out two forces to deal with these under Generals Macpherson and Baker. The latter force was accompanied by 450 rifles of the 5th Punjab Infantry under Major Pratt, and encamped that night at Chihildukhtaran, twelve miles from Kabul, marching next day, the 10th, for Maidan. A hundred rifles under Lieutenant J. P. Sparling formed the bulk of the rearguard, which, owing to the length of the march and the difficulties of the road, was unable to reach camp and had to bivouac in the pass without fires. All suffered severely from the cold, and the rearguard had to fight its way into camp in the morning.

On leaving camp again early on the morning of the 11th for Argandeh, in order to carry out a combined movement with General Macpherson, it was seen that the Afghans were occupying the heights on both flanks of the line of advance.

When the main body had marched and the same rearguard was preparing to leave the ground, the enemy came up from the rear in force and attacked with great vigour with the intention of cutting off Lieutenant Sparling and his men. Another 100 rifles were sent him under Lieutenant Jameson and also two mountain guns, when the enemy was driven off and the column reached Argandeh without further molestation.

In this affair Sepoy Mahammed Yar was killed, and Sepoys Nihal Singh, Sohail Singh (died of wounds), Wasim and Mahammed Ali and Bhisti Bhagu (died of wounds) were wounded. Naik Sarwan Singh was awarded the Order of Merit for gallantry on this occasion.

The combined movement having failed of achievement, General Baker's force fell back on Kabul, followed up for nearly six miles, the Regiment having one man—Sepoy Saif Ali—wounded.

On December 13th the Regiment was broken up into several detachments, a party of 150 rifles under Major Pratt being told off to open up communication with a force then operating outside the city under General Baker. This was duly effected, and in the course of this duty the enemy was found in position and was attacked, driven off and pursued. On this occasion Lieutenant Jameson particularly distinguished himself, killing two of the enemy. Again, on joining General Baker, Major Pratt was ordered to storm a fortified serai occupied by Afghans, who offered a very stout resistance. Ladders were brought to scale the walls of the serai and volunteers to storm were called for. The call was readily responded to, and the serai was attacked over the walls and by the door, which by this had been burnt down. Major Pratt led the assaulting party, but just as he entered the gateway, Havildar Sham Singh rushed past him and received one bullet wound and five sword-cuts from Afghans who attacked him on both sides. In this affair four men were wounded—Havildar Sham Singh (who died of his wounds), Sepoys Kurban Ali, Assa Singh and Awal Khan ; the following were awarded the Order of Merit :—Subadar Baz Gul, Lance-Naiks Akram, Niamat and Man Singh, and Sepoy Umrah.

When, on December 14th, General Baker moved out to attack the enemy on the heights above Deh-Afghana, the Regiment was held in reserve until the close of the operations ; then, the Afghans counter-attacking in great force, our troops were driven in some confusion from a hill they had occupied, and 100 men under Captain Hall and Subadar Juma Khan were sent up to cover the retreat, regaining the hill and falling back so steadily from one position to another, that they effectually prevented the enemy from following up into the plain. The casualties this day were—killed and died of wounds : Naik Ruldu and Sepoys Buddu and Kassim ; wounded : Havildar Harif, Naiks Hussun and Chanda Singh, Sepoys Nur Khan, Eman Bakhsh, Ghanta, Mehtab, Aga Ram, Lal Singh, Kaudu and Hera.

During the siege by the Afghans of the Sherpur Cantonment, which commenced this day and continued until the 23rd, the Regiment was constantly engaged and for part of the time held the King's Garden during these nine days, having two men—Sepoys Kishan Singh and Dewah Singh—killed, and three sepoys—Esar Singh, Sharm Singh and Darbari—wounded.

When the siege was raised and the troops were able again to take the field, the Regiment accompanied the force that at the end of the year visited the Koh-i-Daman ; and in May, 1880, it accompanied the division in its march through the Logar Valley, Wardak and Maidan, returning to Kabul along the valley of the Kabul River—a very rugged and mountainous country, hitherto quite unexplored.

On August 6th the Regiment paraded before Sir F. Roberts, who presented to the Indian officers and men the awards they had earned, and expressed his approbation of the behaviour of all ranks while serving under his command. Two days later General Roberts left Kabul with the force intended for the relief of Kandahar, whither the troops under General Burrows' command had withdrawn after the disastrous defeat at Maiwand.

5th P.I. DEFENCES. SHERPUR, 1880

BRITISH AND INDIAN OFFICERS, 5th P.I., 1889

Meanwhile, during the last week of July, the negotiations which had for some time been proceeding with Sirdar Abdur Rahman, with the view of placing him upon the throne of Kabul, had advanced satisfactorily towards a conclusion ; the news having now been received that he was on his way to Kabul where he was to be proclaimed Amir, it was decided to withdraw the troops from Northern Afghanistan by way of the Khyber, and on August 11th the withdrawal actually commenced.

The 5th Punjab Infantry was the last regiment to leave the Bala Hissar, Lieut.-Colonel McQueen handing over the keys of the fortress to the representative of the new Amir. The return march was without incident of any kind, and the Regiment arrived at Kohat on September 10th, 1880.

The following is a summary of the casualties incurred by the Regiment in the Afghan campaign of 1878-80 :—

	British Officers.	Indian Officers.	N.C.Os.	R. and F.	Followers.	Total.
Killed	—	3	5	21	2	31
Wounded	1	—	5	34	—	40
Died	—	—	11	69	7	87
Total ...	1	3	21	124	9	158

Major J. W. McQueen, Major H. M. Pratt and Captain C. M. Hall of the Regiment were all mentioned in Lieut.-General Sir F. Roberts' despatches, and the first-named was promoted Brevet Lieutenant-Colonel and was awarded the C.B., while the two other officers were promoted Brevet Lieutenant-Colonel and Brevet Major respectively. The awards given to the Indian ranks have for the most part been stated during the course of the foregoing narrative, but in addition to these Subadar-Major Pir Shah and Subadar Juma Khan were admitted to the First and Second Classes of the Order of British India with the rank of Sirdar Bahadur and Bahadur respectively.

In concluding this chapter, it may here be mentioned that the following appeared in G.G.O. No. 418 of July 29th, 1881 :—

" *The Most Honourable the Governor-General in Council announces that Her Majesty the Queen, Empress of India, has been graciously pleased to permit the following Corps to bear upon their Standards, Colours or appointments the words specified below in commemoration of their gallant conduct during the recent campaigns in Afghanistan :—*

* * * * *

" *5th Punjab Infantry*—' *Peiwar Kotal,*' ' *Charasia,*' ' *Kabul,* 1879,' '*Afghanistan,* 1878-80.' "

CHAPTER II

SECOND PERIOD

1881—1914

THE Regiment had been settled down in cantonments again for rather less than five months when, on February 5th, 1881, the 5th Punjab Infantry marched for the Miranzai Valley, the Headquarters halting at Togh, where it formed part of the Kurram Brigade Field Force under General J. Gordon. The Mahsud Wazirs had been concerned with other tribes in several outrages on the Thal—Kurram road and on the Kohat border in 1880, but at that time the Government had its hands sufficiently full with the operations in Afghanistan, and it was not until their close that it was able to take up the case against the Mahsuds

Two columns had been formed, the one, under Brig.-General T. J. Kennedy, C.B., Commanding the Punjab Frontier Force, and who was to be in general charge of the operations, being based on Tank, while the other, described at the outset as a Reserve Brigade, was to operate from Bannu.

On arrival at Togh the Regiment occupied the outposts of Thal, Gundiaur and Surozai until April 16th, when these detachments rejoined Headquarters, and on May 14th General Gordon's column moved off. Advancing by the Khaisora route, Saroba was reached on the 6th, Razani on the 7th and Razmak, in the very heart of the Waziri country, on the 9th; and from here communication was established with the Tank column, then at Kaniguram, and supplies were forwarded to it. After a stay of four days at Razmak, the column returned by the Shaktu Valley, reaching British territory on May 20th. The troops had met with little or no opposition, but were throughout actively employed in making reconnaissances, guarding survey parties, road-making and foraging.

On May 10th 150 rifles of the Regiment with two British officers, the whole forming part of a larger force under Major C. M. Hall, escorted a survey party to the summit of the Shewidhur Mountain, one of the highest peaks in Waziristan, being upwards of 11,000 feet above sea-level. On the next day, while descending the mountain, the force was attacked, when the rearguard, composed of men of the 5th, covered the retreat, suffered no loss themselves and killed five of the enemy, capturing their arms. On this occasion Jemadar Abdul Rahman greatly distinguished himself.

Again, at the end of 1883, the Regiment, being then quartered at Dera Ismail Khan, was called upon for service of a similar nature to the above.

For some five or six years past the Government had been desirous that the Takht-i-Suliman Mountain in the Shirani country should be explored and surveyed, provided that this could be effected without undue risk ; and in this year the majority of the tribe concerned having offered no objection, and, further, having given hostages for maintaining a peaceful attitude while the work was in progress, sanction to the expedition was accorded. On November 14th, 1883, therefore, Head-quarters and 496 bayonets of the 5th Punjab Infantry marched from Dera Ismail Khan to Draband, and joined a mixed force some 1,500 strong which was there assembling under Brig.-General Kennedy. The force crossed the frontier on the 18th, and on the 23rd reached Kach Mazrai, where it was reported that there would probably be opposition two marches in front, at the Pezai Kotal, where some 300 Shiranis had assembled to dispute the passage.

To clear the road two small columns were formed, each of 580 bayonets and the one having four guns attached. On the 26th the neighbourhood of the Pezai Kotal was reached, over which passed the road to the Takht-i-Suliman, and while 180 men of the Regiment under Major C. M. Hall took part in the frontal attack, the same number, commanded by Major A. D. Strettell, joined the right or turning movement, entailing a circuit of some six miles and lasting some six hours. On finding their position turned and their rear threatened, the enemy fled, being followed up in different directions by both columns and incurring some loss.

The survey work was then completed and the Regiment returned on December 8th to Dera Ismail Khan and from here in the following

December it marched in relief to Edwardsabad, where it relieved the 4th Sikhs and was quartered in the Fort Dulipgarh lines in the main fort.

On November 12th of this year application had been made by Colonel A. G. Ross, the officiating Commandant of the Regiment, for permission to send the old Colours to the Lawrence Hall in Lahore for safe keeping. These were the Colours originally issued to the 5th Punjab Infantry in August, 1852, and were of the old large pattern with spear-head poles, as in use until after the Mutiny. The Regiment had never carried these Colours, nor had it replaced them. Sanction to the request made was accorded in Letter No. 101 C. of February 5th, 1885, and the old Colours were duly handed over to the Deputy Commissioner of Lahore for transfer to the Lahore Municipality by Colour-Havildar Hira Singh on March 21st.

At the end of 1884 the attitude of Russia and the advance which, in spite of all engagements to the contrary, she had made towards our Indian frontier and especially in the direction of Afghanistan, had revived mistrust in Russian good faith and caused serious uneasiness to the Indian Government, which had guaranteed protection to the Amir against foreign aggression from any quarter.

The danger of a collision between England and Russia seemed now so menacing, that it was arranged between the two countries that each should dispatch a commission to effect a delimitation of the Afghan frontier on the west. The British commissioner duly arrived at the place agreed upon, but the Russian commissioner delayed his arrival on various pretexts, while the Russian military force on the spot kept pushing on eastward, finally reaching a strong position on the road to Herat, some miles beyond the district previously occupied by Russia. By the middle of January, 1885, the Russian commissioner had still not put in an appearance, and the Russian Government, being pressed on the subject by the British Cabinet, now for the first time declared that a definite zone must be decided upon " before the Commissioners could begin operations."

In the meantime the Russian troops continued to advance, and on March 30th the long expected collision between Russians and Afghans took place, the former attacking the troops of the Amir at Penjdeh, a fortified position on the Kushk River, defeating them with great loss and capturing guns, stores and baggage.

The British Government now made ready for the war which seemed to have become unavoidable. In England Mr. Gladstone, the Premier, asked for a war-vote of eleven millions, and the Army Reserve was called out. In India two Army Corps, each of 25,000 men with a Reserve of 10,000, were mobilized, and reinforcements of British troops to the number of 15,000 were asked for from England. It was considered that the North-West Frontier could not at this crisis be denuded of its best and most experienced troops, and the 5th Punjab Infantry was consequently not detailed for service in either Army Corps, but was called upon to hand over nearly all its regimental transport to the 4th Punjab Infantry and the 1st Sikhs. By the end of May, however, the tension was relaxed and the forces assembled were gradually demobilized.

For the Punjab Frontier Force the year 1886 brought a very great change in regard to its status and method of control, for by G.G.O. No. 485 the Force which, since its creation in 1849 had been under the direct authority of the Government of the Punjab, was brought immediately under that of the Commander-in-Chief in India. In announcing this transfer of authority the G.G.O. stated as follows :—

" *His Excellency in Council is authorized to express the high sense entertained by Her Majesty the Queen Empress of the loyal and brilliant services, which, under the Government of the Province, the Punjab Frontier Force has invariably rendered to the State from the earliest period of its creation . . . The Force will continue as a separate unit, and, as far as practicable, its local and distinctive character will be preserved, its institutions maintained, and its existing privileges continued.*"

In making known this change in Army Orders, General Sir F. Roberts said :—

" *For upwards of thirty-five years the Punjab Frontier Force has been steadily adding to its laurels. Its list of casualties during that time bears testimony to the gallantry and devotion of all ranks in many a hard-fought action, while the admirable manner in which discipline has at all times been maintained, has contributed materially to the high reputation for soldier-like qualities which the Force now so deservedly enjoys.*

N.C.Os. AND MEN, 5th P.I., 1889

INDIAN OFFICERS, 5th P.I., 1893

"*The addition of so distinguished a force to the Bengal Army would, under all circumstances, be a matter of congratulation to the Commander-in-Chief in India; but as a former Commandant of the Punjab Frontier Force it is especially gratifying to Sir Frederick Roberts that this measure has come into operation during his tenure of office.*

"*His Excellency takes this opportunity of assuring the officers, non-commissioned officers and men of the Force that it will be his special privilege, not only to watch over their interests in the future, but to take care that the many customs and traditions which have so largely contributed to make the Force what it is, are interfered with as little as possible. In offering a soldier's welcome to all ranks of the Punjab Frontier Force, Sir Frederick Roberts is sure that he is only giving expression to what is the unanimous feeling throughout the Army of Bengal.*"

The actual transfer took place on August 1st of this year, by which date the Punjab Frontier Force had expanded from its original dimensions to a small army, containing four mountain batteries, one garrison company, five regiments of cavalry, the Corps of Guides, four regiments of Sikh infantry, six regiments of Punjab Infantry and one Gurkha Regiment, numbered the 5th Gurkhas.

By Army Circular of March 31st, 1887, it was directed that the establishment of infantry regiments of the Punjab Frontier Force should for the future be 8 subadars, 8 jemadars, 40 havildars, 40 naiks, 16 drummers and 800 sepoys, being an increase of eighty sepoys over the existing establishment; and by July 14th of this year the Regiment, then at Edwardsabad, had recruited up to its augmented numbers.

On January 17th, 1888, the 5th Punjab Infantry, having by this been just two years at Edwardsabad, marched to Kohat, where it arrived on the 24th and relieved the 2nd Punjab Infantry, occupying the left infantry lines. This was unfortunately to be an unhealthy year for the Regiment, for on August 5th a case of cholera occurred in the lines and the disease increased so rapidly and spread to such an extent among the men, that by the 9th it was considered advisable to move the Regiment out of the lines, and it was accordingly placed under canvas on the parade ground of the 1st Sikh Infantry, remaining here until 6th September. There were in all 42 cases of cholera in the Regiment—35 among the fighting men and 7 among the followers, 21 proving fatal among the former and 5 among the followers.

Subadar-Major Budh Singh was, on September 21st, 1889, admitted to the Second-Class of the Order of British India with the title of Bahadur.

During the cold weather of this year there was renewed trouble with the Jawaki Afridis, a certain firebrand of the name of Mushki endeavouring to cause disaffection ; the result was one of those surprise raids in which the regiments of the Punjab Frontier Force have, by long practice, become past masters, and for which they have earned the respect and admiration even of the raided.

On the night of November 17th—18th 3 British officers, 9 Indian officers and 368 other ranks took part in the surprise of the Jawaki village of Sharidand, which resulted in the capture of Mushki and his followers. There were no casualties, the surprise being complete. The men were under arms for twenty hours, during which they marched twenty-six miles.

By an Army Circular dated April 22nd, 1890, the Regiment was ordered to enlist another company of Afridis, making a ninth company in all.

At the end of this year a large camp of instruction was assembled in the vicinity of Attock, and this was followed by manœuvres of unusual interest and on a large scale, ending up with field-firing with service ammunition by all arms. The Regiment was detailed to attend this camp, and on November 12th marched out from Kohat to Fort Mackeson *en route* to Attock at a strength of 7 British officers, 13 Indian officers, 35 havildars and 509 rank and file, joining at Nowshera on November 15th the 2nd Brigade, Peshawar Force. The force remained in camp until November 4th, when the following congratulatory orders were published :—

From the General Officer Commanding :—

" *The Camp of Instruction being now ended, the General Officer Commanding wishes to place on record his appreciation of the excellent manner in which all ranks behaved on all occasions and the cheerful way they have met the discomforts incidental to bad weather.*"

From General Sir F. S. Roberts, Commander-in-Chief :—

"*The forces concentrated at Attock and Akhora being about to return to quarters, General Officers Commanding Divisions are requested to notify to the officers and men who have taken part in the manœuvres the satisfaction with which the Commander-in-Chief has followed the movements. The troops were assembled with the twofold object of elucidating the facilities for attack and defence offered by the Attock position, and of affording practical experience of the operations of war in a difficult country. The results in both respects have been extremely valuable, and while regretting the curtailment of the manœuvres by inclement weather, His Excellency desires to record his appreciation of the soldierlike keenness and cheerful spirit displayed by all ranks in carrying out their onerous duties. The march of the Akhora Division through the Kunna Khel Pass presented considerable difficulty, and General Keene's subsequent plans were well calculated to ensure the success of his attack.*

"*The field firing with service ammunition carried out on December 2nd by the combined forces, consisting of 9 batteries of artillery, 6 regiments of cavalry and 17 battalions of infantry, representing nearly 16,000 men, was on a larger scale than had been previously attempted, the position was admirably chosen, and the success of the experiment reflects the highest credit on the general steadiness of the men and the excellent arrangements made by the Musketry Staff under the orders of the General Officer Commanding.*

"*In conclusion, the Commander-in-Chief congratulates the General Officers Commanding Divisions and Brigades on the successful issue of the manœuvres and the exemplary conduct of all ranks under their command, not a single complaint affecting any soldier having been received by the civil authorities during the time the troops have been in camp.*"

The Regiment now marched back to Kohat on December 5th by way of Taru, Peshawar and Mattani, arriving at Kohat on the 10th.

It had, however, been back in its peace garrison little more than a month, during which time it was inspected by General Sir W. Lockhart, K.C.B., C.S.I., commanding the Punjab Frontier Force, when on January 12th, 1891, orders were received that it was to take part in the Miranzai Expedition of this year, directed against the

Orakzais, and was to form part of the second column under the command of Lieut.-Colonel A. H. Turner, of the 2nd Punjab Infantry.

For some considerable time past certain sections of the Orakzais had given persistent trouble, and it had been decided to occupy the whole of their country up to the foot of the Samana Range, while further it was agreed that there was no chance of any permanent settlement of this part of the border without a punitive expedition. On January 2nd, therefore, the Government of India ordered an expedition to be dispatched, with the special object of punishing and enforcing the submission of the four Samil sections of the Orakzais, *viz.*: the Rabia Khel, Sheikhan, Mishti and Mamuzai, as well as the Sturi Khel, should these latter not submit when the Khanki Valley was occupied.

The force to be employed contained 2 squadrons of cavalry, 2 mountain batteries and 9 battalions of infantry. It was divided into three columns, and in the third column with the 5th Punjab Infantry were No. 3 Peshawar Mountain Battery, half a company of Bengal Sappers and the 2nd Punjab Infantry. On January 12th the Regiment received its orders and left Kohat two days later for Sherkot in the Miranzai Valley, a depot remaining behind under the command of Captain F. P. L. White.

The marching-out strength of the 5th Punjab Infantry was 8 British officers, 13 Indian officers, 37 havildars, 13 buglers and 538 rank and file. The British officers were Lieut.-Colonel A. D. Strettell (in command), Captain R. F. Jameson, F. B. Thein and L. E. Cooper, Lieutenants A. A. J. Johnstone (Adjutant), R. C. O. Creagh (Quartermaster), and W. E. Venour and Surgeon C. E. Sunder (Medical Officer).

The column had to halt at Ibrahimzai owing to the extreme inclemency of the weather, and the men experienced the greatest discomfort from frost and cold, while the fields where the Regiment was encamped were flooded, being over ankle-deep in mud and slush, so that the men had to sleep on wet ground. After a four days' halt the column marched for Togh under great difficulties, owing to the weather, and on arrival had again to camp on wet fields. On January 20th, 1891, the Regiment furnished a working party of 2 Indian officers and 75 rifles to help make the Darband road, while an Indian officer and 50 men under Lieutenant Creagh was sent to reconnoitre the road leading from Pat Darband up to the Samani Ghar into the Khanki Valley.

On this day Lieutenant W. V. Manning, 4th Sikhs, was attached for duty.

During the five days the Regiment remained here it furnished working and covering parties on the Darband road, and then on the 25th it marched with the Brigade to Darband, and next day over the Pat Darband Pass to camp at Saifal Darra. No camel transport was taken, and even for mules the descent on the further side of the Pass was very difficult; while as rain again fell heavily and persistently the men got very wet and camp was not finally reached till 9 p.m.

That night the Regiment supplied four picquets to east and west of the camp, each of twelve rifles.

On January 27th two companies of the Regiment with the men on picquet and two companies of the 2nd Punjab Infantry, the whole under Lieutenant Venour, were ordered to move with the baggage and transport down the Saifal Darra Valley and then up the Khanki Valley towards Gwada, there joining the first column which was marching from the Latra Valley. For the remainder of the second column the following orders were issued:—The 2nd Punjab Infantry with the sappers were to climb a hill on the left near the mouth of the Darra, while the 5th Punjab Infantry was to make a detour and meet the 2nd Punjab Infantry on the top of the spur. This junction was duly effected after a difficult climb of about an hour and a half, and the Regiment then extended for attack, two companies under Captain Mcin in front, two under Captain Jameson in support and the rest in reserve; and then, the 2nd Punjab Infantry following, an advance was made against the village of Sarmala. The Orakzai villages were all found to be deserted and five of them were destroyed by the first and second columns. The force then withdrew unmolested, the second column fording the Khanki stream and camping near the village of Jandasam, the Regiment providing three picquets for the protection of the camp.

On the 29th Captain Cooper took a reconnoitring party into the Shaik Khan country, and next day the Regiment was transferred to the third column and moved on February 1st to Hangu, when this column was broken up and the Regiment left on the 4th for Kohat, arriving there next day and relieving the 22nd Punjab Infantry, which had occupied the lines during its absence.

At the end of the first week in March the 5th moved in relief to Dera Ismail Khan and arrived there on the 23rd, but on April 13th was ordered off again to Edwardsabad to take the place there of the 6th Punjab Infantry, which was leaving to take part in another expedition into the Miranzai Valley which had now become necessary. The Regiment remained in Edwardsabad from April 19th to June 14th, when it returned to Dera Ismail Khan.

On September 18th of this year the Regiment was re-armed with Martini-Henry rifles in lieu of Sniders.

In February, 1892, the Amir of Afghanistan began, not for the first time, to intrigue with the Mahsud Wazirs, and in May one of his Sirdars appeared at Wana with a force of cavalry and infantry. Repeated, but apparently ineffectual, warnings were addressed to the Amir by the Supreme Government, and in July the Mahsud maliks petitioned the Government that the post at Khajuri Kach might be strengthened, as the Sirdar was trying to stir up trouble and it was necessary to keep the discontented men of the tribe in check. It was now decided that additional troops should be concentrated in Waziristan, and on July 29th a detachment of the Regiment under Captain Cooper—160 all ranks—left to join a column which proceeded to Khajuri Kach. On September 22nd the remainder of the Regiment also marched off to join the Wana Field Force, composed of a squadron of cavalry, six guns and three infantry battalions, and before this display of strength the Amir now withdrew his troops from the country; but it was not until April 25th, 1893, that the Regiment finally left Khajuri Kach on its return march to Dera Ismail Khan. Here the Corps remained until January of the year following when it changed quarters to Kohat.

In the autumn of this year the Regiment received, with great regret, the news of the death at Bedford on August 29th of its first commandant, General James Eardley Gastrell. On May 27th of the year 1896 this was followed by the announcement of the death at Tunbridge Wells of Colonel C. Mackenzie Hall, who had served for twenty-four years in the 5th Punjab Infantry.

During the early summer of 1897 reliable reports came to hand that certain of the Afridis and Orakzais had approached the Amir of Afghanistan with a view to his intervention in securing the evacuation of the Samana by our troops; and while the general situation in this part of the border was considered to be serious, it was thought unlikely that these tribes would really commit themselves to any outstanding acts of hostility. At this time, and until late in the summer, troops were disposed as follows in the immediate neighbourhood.

At Kohat were 4 mountain guns, 2 squadrons of cavalry and the 2nd and 5th Punjab Infantry.

At Parachinar were 2 mountain guns, 2 squadrons of cavalry, a wing of the 5th Gurkhas and 250 rifles of the 36th Sikhs. On the Samana was the remainder of the 36th Sikhs.

On August 15th the garrison of Kohat was increased by the arrival of the 9th Field Battery, R.A., the 18th Bengal Lancers and the 15th Sikhs, and a flying column, composed of 4 mountain guns, the 18th Bengal Lancers, 2 squadrons 3rd Punjab Cavalry and the 5th Punjab Infantry, under Colonel G. Richardson, C.I.E., was now formed and on the 21st marched to Hangu. The following British officers accompanied the Regiment:—Lieut.-Colonel R. F. Jameson (in command), Major F. P. L. White, Captain P. Holland, Lieutenants R. W. E. Knollys (Adjutant), F. P. James (Quartermaster), A. G. Ames (Transport Officer) and Surgeon-Lieutenant C. H. Watson.

On August 25th Lieut.-Colonel Jameson with 500 of his own men and two guns marched to the forts on the Samana, taking a fresh supply of ammunition for the garrisons, which had not so far been attacked. It was ascertained that 1,000 tribesmen were watching the movements of the convoy, while it was also learnt that day that a *lashkar* of 12,000 tribesmen was concentrating at Kharappa in the Khanki Valley; but Colonel Jameson's force returned, uninterfered with, to camp before dusk, having marched in all twenty-eight miles.

There was some fighting about the Ublan Pass on the 26th, and next day matters on the Samana assumed a more serious aspect, early in the morning the post of Lakka, held by local levies, being surrounded and attacked, when the garrison signalled for assistance. Colonel Richardson immediately sent off a mixed force of 2 guns, a troop of cavalry, the 15th Sikhs and a wing of the 5th Punjab Infantry—the latter under Major White, with orders to relieve Lakka and the post at Saifal Darra, which was also threatened. The column left Hangu at 9 a.m., and began the ascent up the graded road to Lakka, the enemy nowhere appearing in large numbers, but taking every advantage of cover and keeping up a tolerably hot fire. When the column had ascended the hill about halfway, the enemy managed to enfilade the road so successfully that the infantry was now obliged to leave it and move directly up the *khud*. The ground was most difficult, but, never halting, the troops went straight on, swept away all opposition, and gained the crest in remarkably short time, the enemy melting away to the north and east.

Colonel Abbott, commanding the column, now moved on to relieve Lakka, and the wing of the 5th was ordered to keep the enemy in check while this was being done; and thereafter he pushed on to relieve Saifal Darra, also reported to be hard-pressed, the wing of the Regiment acting as rearguard.

In the meantime the Headquarter Wing of the Regiment, accompanied by Colonel Richardson, had moved up to the foot of the hills ready to cover Colonel Abbott's retirement, and this column being seen falling back about 7 p.m., Colonel Jameson's wing now moved straight up the spurs covering the zigzag road for some thousand feet. The ascent was extraordinarily difficult, over very jagged rocks and huge fissures, and the men were much exhausted by the time the last position to be held was reached. The enemy followed up, but was checked, and one body of fifty, attempting a charge, lost severely. They got, however, to fairly close quarters, and Subadar Man Singh, already wounded, had to use sword and revolver, cutting one man down from the shoulders.

Camp was reached about 11 p.m., the men having had no food and very little water. One man—Sepoy Phula—was killed, Subadar Man Singh wounded, and two sepoys were missing, but these came in next day.

Both Colonels Richardson and Abbott expressed themselves as greatly pleased with the behaviour of the Regiment, and the services of Subadar-Major Wazir Khan and Subadar Passand Khan were specially brought to notice.

It was now considered necessary to arrange for the protection of the frontier further to the west, and on August 30th Colonel Richardson sent a small force to Doaba, twenty-two miles to the west of Hangu; and on September 1st, information having come in that an attack upon Sadda and Parachinar was projected—Sadda being seventy and Parachinar ninety-two miles distant—he directed the force sent to Doaba to push on to the relief of Sadda, while he moved with the remainder of the troops at hand—including the 5th Punjab Infantry—on Doaba. The march thither was a very trying one, the heat terrific, and the march greatly delayed by very inefficient transport. The rearguard did not get in until 2 a.m., having been fired into *en route*, but two of the snipers were captured by Subadar Bhan Singh in command of the rearguard.

Early next day Colonel Richardson pushed on with the cavalry to Thal, followed at 8 a.m. by the 5th Punjab Infantry and the guns; this also was a trying march, the men having had but little rest. Thal was, however, reached at 1 p.m., Alizai on the 4th and Sadda on the 5th in pelting rain. Here camp was pitched on a plateau to the north-east, about a mile south-west of the Khurmana defile.

Here everything was quiet until September 16th, when about 10.30 p.m. some 2,000 Massuzais, who had collected in the defile, suddenly attacked the camp. The advanced picquets of the Regiment, in a *sangar* about a hundred yards to the south-east, were driven in by a sudden rush of the tribesmen; the portion of the camp next attacked was the east face held partly by the 5th Gurkhas and partly by the 5th Punjab Infantry, the face held by the Gurkhas being kept engaged by several hundreds of the enemy, while the main attack fell upon the south-east corner held by the Regiment. Finding the camp could not be rushed, the enemy settled down to a well-sustained rifle fire which he kept up for some two and three-quarter hours. The 5th had Havildar Boram Ali killed, while gallantly superintending the retirement of his picquet, and Sepoy Shah Sowar was wounded in three places.

Havildar Juma and Lance-Naik Sher Jung were brought to notice for specially good work, while Surgeon-Lieutenant Watson and Hospital Assistant Durbari Lal afforded medical aid to the wounded under tolerably heavy fire.

Already on September 3rd orders had been issued for the concentration of a force some 44,000 strong for an advance into Tirah in view of the attitude which the Afridis had taken up, involving a general conflagration along some 300 miles of frontier.

The 5th Punjab Infantry did not, however, form part of the Expeditionary Force detailed, in view of Commander-in-Chief's G.O. No. 635 of October 8th, 1897, which ran as follows :—

"*The Afridi soldiers in the service of the Government have given proofs of their loyalty, devotion and courage on many a hard-fought field, and the value of their services has been fully appreciated by the Government of India. After the most careful consideration of the circumstances connected with the Tirah Expedition, the Government has decided to show consideration to the Afridi soldiers who wish to keep their engagement and to excuse them from service which the Government has been forced to wage against their fellow-tribesmen. On these grounds alone it has been determined that Afridi soldiers who are serving in the regiments detailed for service on the Peshawar—Kohat border are not to be employed near the Tirah frontier at the present time, but their services will be utilized elsewhere.*

"*The necessary orders to this effect will at once issue. As far as possible care will be taken that the property of those who have not taken part in the raids on British territory is neither confiscated nor destroyed during the time that our troops are engaged in the Orakzai or Afridi country.*

"*This order is to be read and carefully explained to all Afridi soldiers belonging to regiments detailed for service on the Peshawar—Kohat border.*"

In March, 1898, the Regiment learnt with great regret of the death by assassination at Smallan, near Dukhi in Baluchistan, of Lieut.-Colonel Gaisford, Deputy Commissioner of Quetta and Pishin, who had joined the Punjab Frontier Force in 1870 and took part with the Regiment in the Jawaki Expedition and the Second Afghan War.

The following announcements appeared in Orders this year :—

"Her Majesty was pleased to confer on Subadar Zaman Ali,* 5th Punjab Infantry, permission to wear the Order of the Brilliant Star of Zanzibar conferred in recognition of active and distinguished service before the enemy."

* Subadar Zaman Ali and eleven sepoys of the Regiment rejoined this year at the expiration of three years' service in East Africa for which they had volunteered.

" Sepoy Mohan Singh, 5th Punjab Infantry, was admitted to the Order of Merit for conspicuous gallantry while attached to the 36th Sikhs at Fort Cavagnari on September 13th, 1897."

During the greater part of 1899 the Regiment was quartered at Wana, moving to Edwardsabad in December of that year. While at Wana the men suffered severely from malarial fever, due to the nature of the country and the heavy convoy and night duty which all ranks were called upon to perform. Then, very soon after reaching Edwardsabad there was an epidemic of pneumonia, and during the first five months of the year 1900 no fewer than forty-three deaths occurred in the Regiment, mainly due to this disease. Following closely upon this, cholera of an unusually severe type broke out, occasioning the deaths of two fighting men and of one of the transport followers.

In the spring of this year H.E. the Viceroy visited Edwardsabad, and on April 21st the 5th Punjab Infantry found a Guard of Honour for him of one British officer—Lieutenant Thomson—2 Indian officers and 100 rank and file, on the occasion of his arrival at the Deputy Commissioner's bungalow in the morning, and again in the evening at the Punjab Frontier Force Mess; also a guard over the bungalow during his stay of 2 Indian officers and 80 rank and file. The *Pioneer* of April 23rd described the Guard of Honour as " one of the smartest inspected by His Excellency on this tour."

Since the middle of 1898 there had been a recrudescence of outrages by the Mahsud Wazirs in British territory and within the protected area of southern Waziristan. During 1898 and 1899 raids were frequent and in January, 1900, the Levy Post at Zam and the Public Works Department bungalow at Murtaza were both attacked. Eventually it was decided that the punishment of the tribe must be undertaken for the fourth time, this taking the form of a blockade to come into operation on December 1st, 1900. To assist to this end the Regiment proceeded to the Tochi Valley on October 1st, 1900, at a strength of 600 rifles with the following British officers :—Lieut.-Colonels Jameson and White, Captain Johnstone, Lieutenants James, Thomson, Gilchrist and Lind, and Captain Newman, I.M.S. On arrival in the Tochi Valley, the Regiment relieved the 4th Sikhs at Miranshah, where it remained for a year, and then, on December 29th, 1901, moved *via*

Boya to Datta Khel, where it arrived on the following day. The 5th Punjab Infantry now contained only 430 Indian ranks, with Lieut.-Colonel White, Majors Johnstone and Creagh, Lieutenants Davidson-Houston, Brown and Smith, and Captain Anderson, I.M.S.

At Datta Khel the Regiment came under Colonel Tonnochy, 3rd Sikhs, who was in command of a column of some 1,400 men, one of three columns formed to act against and punish the Shabi Khel and other Mahsud sections, having settlements in the Shaktu, Sheranna and Shuza Algads. The three columns were based on Jandola, Jani Khel and Datta Khel respectively. No. 3, Colonel Tonnochy's column, consisted of the 1st Bn. 2nd Gurkhas, 2nd Punjab Infantry and 5th Punjab Infantry, with two mountain guns. No. 3 column left Datta Khel on January 1st, 1902, and moved to Wachfakiram and Waladin, proceeding thence to Kikarai. On the 5th the defences of certain villages in the Tank Zam were destroyed, and on the 6th, being joined by No. 2 column, the combined forces moved up the Shaktu and destroyed thirteen tribal towers. In these operations two men of the 5th Punjab Infantry were wounded—No. 2157 Sepoy Farangi and No. 1929 Sepoy Atta Mahammed.

The two columns then retired on Datta Khel, where they arrived on January 8th, and from here the Regiment marched by way of Boya to Miranshah, which was reached on the 10th.

Four hundred and fifteen rifles of the Regiment, with 10 Indian and 6 British officers—Major Creagh, Captain Thomson, Lieutenants Baldwin, Elliot and Finlay, and Lieutenant Illius, I.M.S.—were employed with a small column operating from Idak in the operations carried out in November, 1902, against the Kabul Khel branch of the Darwesh Khel Wazirs. There was little opposition, and the country was traversed in all directions and much damage inflicted on the tribesmen; the Regiment was back at Miranshah by the 27th of the month.

Captain Davidson-Houston of the Regiment was wounded during these operations, while attached to the 4th Sikhs.

From Miranshah the Regiment marched in February via Bannu and Kohat to Khushalgarh, where it entrained for Rawal Pindi, which place was reached on the night of March 8th.

In this year the Indian Army was wholly re-organized, and some changes of great and far-reaching importance were inaugurated.

Lord Kitchener, fresh from bringing the campaign in South Africa to an end, had taken up the appointment of Commander-in-Chief in India on November 28th, 1902, and at once began to consider and frame a scheme for the re-organization and re-distribution of the Army. Under G.G.O. No. 1 of 1903 the designation " Indian Staff Corps " was abolished, and that of " Indian Army " substituted ; while by G.G.O No. 237 of March 2nd the Punjab Frontier Force ceased to exist as a separate body. Later, the Army in India was divided into three Army Corps, a Northern, a Western and an Eastern ; and finally in Indian Army Order No. 181 of October 2nd, certain new designations and numbers of all units of the Indian Army were published, to have effect from the date of the order. In this Army Order all regiments were numbered in one sequence according to their arms—except Gurkha battalions—and all mention of the designations of the old Presidency armies was omitted.

Under this new scheme the 5th Punjab Infantry was for the future to be known as and entitled " the 58th Vaughan's Rifles (Frontier Force)," to be linked with the 55th and 57th Rifles, and the regimental centre being at Dera Ismail Khan.

In a Punjab Frontier Force Order of March 31st, Major-General Sir Charles Egerton, K.C.B., D.S.O., A.D.C., Commanding the Frontier Force and Frontier District, recounted the past glorious services of the Force during its fifty-four years of honourable existence, and bade all ranks a regretful farewell.

During this cold weather the Regiment was sent up to Chakdarra, beyond the Malakand, to cover the movements of the Chitral reliefs, leaving Chakdarra again on October 26th and marching back to Rawal Pindi through the Yusafzai country *via* Ismaila, Maonerai, Kota, Kunda and Torderah, and arriving back at its headquarters by November 11th, the marching-in strength being 7 British officers, 10 Indian officers and 536 other ranks, several Pathan recruits having enlisted *en route*.

On May 13th, 1904, General Sir J. L. Vaughan, K.C.B., was appointed Honorary Colonel of the Regiment.

During this winter the Regiment was again sent up to the Yusafzai border while the Chitral reliefs were moving to and fro.

From December 5th to the 7th, 1905, the 58th Rifles took part in the manœuvres held in the neighbourhood of Jani-ki-Sang before H.R.H. The Prince of Wales, who visited India during this cold weather, and were also present at the Royal Review which took place on Kauna Plain on the 8th of the month, when some 50,000 troops were on parade. The Regiment formed the 5th Brigade, 2nd Division, under Colonel H. B. Watkis, with the 25th and 30th Punjabis and the 56th Infantry (Frontier Force).

In October, 1906, the Regiment made a change of station, moving from Rawal Pindi to Kohat, and remaining at this latter station an unusually long time, for it was not relieved until February 27th, 1910, when it marched to Hangu, leaving a detachment of 230 rifles at Fort Lockhart and another of 80 rifles at Thal. On moving to Hangu, however, it was intimated that the stay of the 58th here was likely to be a comparatively brief one, as it was intended shortly to move the Regiment to Quetta.

On March 9th, 1910, Subadar Zard Ali received at Thal from the hands of Lord Minto, the Viceroy, the Second Class of the Order of British India.

At this time a green merino " Bumble," one and a half inches high and three inches wide, was taken into wear, to be worn in the front of the helmet above the *paggri*.

General Sir J. L. Vaughan, G.C.B., the Honorary Colonel of the Regiment, died at Tunbridge Wells on January 2nd, 1911,

The long-deferred move of the Regiment from Hangu to Quetta at last took place at the beginning of this year, the advance-party under Captain Willis, D.S.O., moving off to Kohat early in February, proceeding thence by train, and being followed on the 17th by the headquarters of the Regiment, which on this day set out on its 520 miles' march to Quetta. The Fort Lockhart and the Thal detachments joined at Doaba, when the marching strength of the 58th Rifles was 12 British officers, 10 Indian officers, 768 rank and file and 48 public followers. The march from Thal to Idak was by Spin Wam, and thence by Murtaza, Mir Ali Khel—the country hereabouts very difficult, the marches varying from fifteen to twenty-two miles—then by Kajuri Kach, where rain fell, to Moghal Kot. After this the road, which had run along the side of the cliff above the Zhob River, was found to have been washed away, and a new road had to be made before the Regiment could proceed on its way. Marching on by Mir Ali Khel, Brunj, Fort Sandeman, Murgha, Loralai, Spiragha and Khanozai, Quetta was finally reached on April 1st, and the Regiment took over the Sandeman Lines from the 124th Baluch Infantry. The march had been a very wet one, with much rain, sleet and even snow.

Green putties were now taken into wear for all ranks in place of the khaki putties hitherto worn.

On September 20th, 1911, a political mission was sent from Quetta to Kharan, on the edge of the Baluchistan desert and some sixty miles from Kalat, the object being to reinstate the son of the late Khan, who had fled to Quetta on the murder of his father by his uncle. The troops accompanying the mission consisted of a mountain battery and the 106th Hazara Pioneers, but thirteen signallers of the 58th Rifles were also sent to assist in the maintenance of communication with Nushki, the nearest telegraph station and some ninety miles from Kharan; these were in charge of Captain Lind. The object of the mission being achieved with little or no opposition, the troops returned to Quetta at the end of October.

It was noted in the *Gazette of India* under the date of December 12th, that Subadar-Major Mir Alam, 58th Rifles, was admitted to the Second Class Order of British India, from that date, with the title of Bahadur.

There is no outstanding event to chronicle during the next three years while the Regiment remained quartered at Quetta, and on March 30th, 1914, it moved to Chaman with a detachment of one Indian officer and 73 rifles at Shelabagh. Shortly after the arrival at this new station the Regiment learnt of the death at Tank on April 12th of Captain G. B. Brown of the 58th, as the result of wounds inflicted by a Mahsud orderly.

The time was now come when the 58th Rifles were to take part in the greatest of all wars, waged in a country of which few of the soldiers composing the Regiment can have known much, if anything, even by hearsay, and carried out under conditions wholly different to those which the most seasoned warrior of them all had ever experienced.

Of the causes of the war, and of the events which led up to it, the following brief mention must suffice. The heir to the throne of Austria-Hungary was murdered on June 28th, but although the Dual Monarchy did not present its ultimatum to the Serbian Government until July 23rd, within a fortnight of this last date the whole of Europe was at war. The statesmen of Great Britain had done all that was possible to prevent, or at least to localize, hostilities, and in England at any rate all had hoped and believed that even at the eleventh hour peaceful counsels might prevail. But no sooner was war declared upon Germany than there came from all quarters of the world evidences of United Empire.

From no part of the British Empire did the call to arms receive a readier response than from India. The Princes buckled on their swords ; upwards of seven hundred of the mightiest among them placed the whole of their resources—their treasuries, their troops, their lives—at the disposal of the King-Emperor, and India's wonderful and whole-hearted answer at once dispelled the Kaiser's foolish dream of revolt in the East.

Already some months previously the Indian Government had been consulted as to the extent to which Indian troops could co-operate in the event of a war between Great Britain and a European Power, and it had been virtually agreed that India should under such circumstances furnish a contingent of two—possibly three—infantry divisions and a cavalry brigade. On August 6th, 1914, the Cabinet proposed to the Indian Government the sending of two infantry divisions and a cavalry brigade to Egypt, with the ultimate end of employing these in Europe ; and the 3rd (Lahore) and 7th (Meerut) Divisions—called simply the Lahore and Meerut Divisions, to avoid confusion with the British formations—and the Secunderabad Cavalry Brigade were selected for Egypt. Finally, on August 27th the decision was come to to use the Indian troops in Europe.*

" In India the first week of August, 1914, was full of vague and alarming rumours. It was not until the 8th that any definite military

* Official History, " France and Belgium," Vol. I, pp. 13 and 14.

orders arrived. On that day the Lahore (3rd Indian War) Division under Lieut.-General H. B. B. Watkis, C.B., received orders to mobilize. The news was received with the wildest enthusiasm by all ranks."*

On August 12th the Regiment, which was then in the 2nd Brigade of the 4th Quetta Division, received telegraphic orders to mobilize as part of the Meerut Division. Men on leave and on furlough were immediately recalled and reservists summoned to rejoin. Lieut.-Colonel Venour, who had been officiating as commander of the 2nd Brigade at Quetta, came back and resumed command of the Regiment on the 15th. Captain A. A. Smith and Lieutenant J. O. Nicholls were detailed for duty at the Depot temporarily formed at Chaman, but intended to move shortly to Multan, and several officers being at home on leave in England, two others were posted for duty—Lieutenants J. M. Craig, 57th Rifles, Frontier Force, and R. A. Reilly, 31st Punjabis.

On September 4th, 1914, the Regiment left Chaman in two trains, reached Karachi on the morning of the 6th and went into camp for some days, while the Division was concentrating and the transports and convoy were being got ready. The 58th now found itself in what had been numbered the 21st, but what was now to be known as the Bareilly Brigade, commanded by Major-General F. Macbean, C.V.O., C.B., and containing, besides the 58th, the 2nd Bn. The Black Watch, the 41st Dogras and the 2nd Bn. 8th Gurkhas.

On September 16th the Regiment embarked, headquarters and five companies in the *Erinpura*, and the remaining three in the *Aronda*, the embarking strength being 12 British officers, 17 Indian officers and 809 non-commissioned officers and men. The names of the British officers were Lieut.-Colonel W. E. Venour, Major A. G. Thomson, Captains A. G. Lind, E. S. C. Willis, D.S.O., C. H. Elliot, S. B. Pope, and W. McM. Black (Adjutant), Lieutenants J. H. Milligan, J. O. Nicolls, J. M. Craig and R. A. Reilly, with Lieutenant S. Gordon, I.M.S. (Medical Officer).

The Indian officers embarking with the Regiment were :—Subadar-Major Mir Alam Bahadur, Subadars Tika Khan, Gujar Singh, Wassan Singh, Phuman Singh, Gokul, Abdul Ali, Saiyid Gul, and Jemadars

* Mereweather and Smith, " The Indian Corps in France," p. 9.

Khan Bahadur, Hira Singh, Saiyid Razam, Wazir Singh, Suba, Harnam Singh, Hamid Khan, Abdul Rahman and Mir Mast.

It was not, however, until September 21st that the fleet of transport sailed for what was still an "unknown destination," escorted by the cruisers *Dartmouth* and *Hardinge* of the Royal Indian Marine.

BRITISH OFFICERS, 58th (VAUGHAN'S) RIFLES (F.F.), 1912

BRITISH OFFICERS, 58th (VAUGHAN'S) RIFLES (F.F.). WAZIRISTAN, 1921

CHAPTER III

Third Period

The Great War, 1914—1920

On the afternoon of September 24th a large convoy of ships was sighted, and these proved to contain the remainder of the Meerut Division which had embarked at Bombay, and the whole now formed a single armada of some forty vessels, escorted by six armed ships of the Royal Navy. The *Emden* and the *Königsberg* were still at large, and the convoy, in order to keep concentrated, had to proceed at the speed of the slowest ship, which could not do more than eight knots an hour. Aden was passed on the night of September 27th, Suez was reached on the 2nd and Port Said on October 3rd.

Leaving Port Said on the 6th, Marseilles was arrived at by dawn on the 11th, and next day the various transports began to enter the docks, proceeding at once with the disembarkation of the troops they carried. On landing the first thing to be done was to issue new rifles, as those brought from India did not take the recently introduced cartridge. Then at 5 p.m. on the 12th the 58th Rifles marched to camp at La Valentine, some eight miles east of the port, and on the morning of the 19th returned in torrential rain to Marseilles—less the Afridi Company, which, having developed some cases of chicken-pox, remained behind in a segregation camp for a fortnight under Captain Lind—and arrived two days later at Orleans, where it remained for the best part of a week in a camp at Cercotte, being fitted out with new serge clothing and pack equipment.

At Port Said, Major C. E. D. Davidson-Houston and Lieutenant L. Gaisford had rejoined from leave in England.

The Indian Army Corps, under Lieut.-General Sir J. Willcocks, had landed in the theatre of war just after the British Army had been transferred from the Aisne to the left of the Allied line, and had commenced the forward movement which closed with the first battle of

Ypres. With the arrival in France of the Meerut Division, the Indian Corps was tolerably complete; two brigades of the Lahore Division had disembarked at Marseilles at the end of September, while the third brigade had been temporarily detained in Egypt to reinforce the garrison pending the arrival of Territorial troops; the Meerut Division had also now landed, while the cavalry of the Corps was on the point of arriving; but at the time when the Lahore Division reached the front the situation was such that several of its battalions were taken from their brigades and thrown in wherever the pressure was greatest, to help stem the German rush between Ypres and La Bassée.

Leaving Orleans by train on the night of October 26th, the Regiment detrained near Hazebrouck at noon on the 28th and marched from thence to Gorre, where part of the Bareilly Brigade was at once taken to relieve British troops in the trenches, the 58th being in Brigade Reserve. The Indian Corps had now taken over the front previously held by the IInd Army Corps; this line was some eight miles in length, beginning at Givenchy on the right and passing through Festubert, Richebourg l'Avoué and Mauquissart to Rouges Bancs on the left. The Meerut Division held the southern portion of the line in the following order from right to left:—the Bareilly Brigade, the Garhwal Brigade, the Dehra Dun Brigade.

Within twenty-four hours of its arrival at the front, the Regiment was to receive its baptism of fire in the Great War. On the afternoon of the 30th information was received that the 2nd Bn. 8th Gurkhas on the left of the Brigade had been very heavily attacked, and had been shelled out of its trenches which had been occupied by the enemy, suffering many casualties, including eight British officers. Orders were given that the captured trenches were to be retaken by half a battalion each of the Bedfordshire and West Riding Regiments, supported by half battalions of the 58th Rifles and 107th Pioneers. For some reason the attack by the two British regiments did not materialize, and at 2.30 a.m. on October 31st the 58th was called upon to pass through the troops in front and rush the trenches. When Major Davidson-Houston and Captain Black went forward to reconnoitre, the latter was shot through the head and killed, but on the Regiment advancing the majority of the enemy evacuated the trenches, the few who stood their ground falling before the bayonets of the 58th Rifles. Steps were at once taken to meet any possible counter-attack, but none was made.

At daybreak Lieut.-Colonel Venour was killed while looking over the parapet to examine the ground in his front.

The Regiment hung on tenaciously all day in its very exposed position in wholly inadequate trenches, exposed to a continuous shelling and fire from trench mortars and rifle grenades; and when at midnight it was relieved by the 41st Dogras and marched back to bivouacs at Gorre, it had sustained the loss of another British officer—Lieutenant J. M. Craig, who was mortally wounded—and had 5 Indian ranks killed, 4 Indian officers and 79 other ranks wounded, many severely.

Major Davidson-Houston now assumed command of the Regiment, and Lieutenant Milligan took over the Adjutancy.

On November 4th the 58th moved to Festubert and occupied some 400 yards of trenches on the extreme left of the right section of the Meerut Division front, and remained in this part of the line until the 24th. These trenches, though terribly water-logged, were deep and narrow and consequently fairly safe, which was just as well, since in places the Germans were only thirty to eighty yards distant, and their snipers, armed with rifles having telescopic sights and stationed behind iron loopholes, were continually on the look-out for a target.

On November 9th the Afridi Company rejoined from Marseilles; and on the 12th Captains H. C. Baldwin and G. S. Bull, who were on leave in England when war broke out and had been employed in training the new armies, rejoined their Regiment.

On November 23rd, the day before the Regiment was relieved at the front, the enemy had pushed up his sap to within five yards of part of the Indian Corps line and then commenced a very violent attack, whereby the 9th Bhopal Infantry and 34th Pioneers were driven out of their trenches; while early on the morning of the 24th "some of the 58th Rifles on the left of the right section of the defence were forced out of their trench and affairs began to look critical. . . . Before evacuating their trenches the 58th had gone through a trying time. Lieutenant Reilly had been killed in a gallant and successful attempt to carry bombs and ammunition up to the firing line. Havildar Hawindah immediately took out a party under a very heavy fire and brought his body in, having already rescued a mortally-wounded havildar. . . . Captain Baldwin found a ditch, in which he held on with great determination, but he was killed later in a counter-attack. The command of the company was then taken by Havildar Indar Singh, who held the position against heavy attacks until relieved next morning. . . . Captain Willis was wounded in the head by a bomb at noon, but continued to command his men, and was finally ordered out of action after taking part in the counter-attack in the afternoon. Captain Lind's company was heavily bombed and enfiladed by a machine gun, with the result that it lost nearly seventy-five per cent of its strength, including its gallant commander.

" Captain Bull had been sent up to relieve the wounded Captain Willis, who, however, declined to be relieved. Captain Bull then got into a ditch with a few men of the 58th and Black Watch, and there they held out with grim determination, stopping the German advance with their fire, although they were heavily bombed from a distance of fifteen yards ; the bombing stopped and the position was secured.

" There is little doubt that Colonel Southey's action on the left and Captain Bull's on the right saved the situation for us, for had they been less determined in holding their ground at all costs, the whole of this section of our line must have fallen into the hands of the enemy."*

At 4.30 p.m. a general counter-attack, led by Major Davidson-Houston in person, was launched under a most effective artillery bombardment, what remained of the Regiment, moving straight on the lost trenches, carried all before them, and regained the position with small loss to themselves and taking a number of German prisoners.

So ended for the 58th Rifles the Battle of Festubert, in which the Regiment had 3 British officers, 1 Indian officer and 42 other ranks killed, 2 British officers, 1 Indian officer and 61 other ranks wounded, and 11 men missing.

On December 7th the Corps Commander issued an order of the day in which he said he had " learnt with great satisfaction of the conduct of the troops engaged under General Egerton, and that the steadiness of the Black Watch and the portion of the 58th Rifles next to them, and especially the flank attack by the 1st Bn. 39th Garhwal

* " The Indian Corps in France," pp. 118-120.

Rifles, which helped to regain the lost trenches, merited special mention."

The Regiment was now relieved and went back to billets at Essars until December 3rd ; and from here on the 1st a party of 2 Indian officers and 100 non-commissioned officers and men, under Captain Bull, marched to Locon where, with other units of the Brigade, it was inspected by His Majesty The King, who was accompanied by H.R.H. The Prince of Wales.

For rather over a fortnight now the Regiment was alternately in bivouac in rear or in the trenches in front, and during this time reinforcements reached the 58th from India, consisting of both British officers and Indian ranks. Captain A. A. Smith of the Regiment joined from the Depot, and the following also reported their arrival :— Captains M. A. Bell, 54th Sikhs, F. F. Hodgson, 84th Punjabis, P. Hore, 52nd Sikhs and D. G. Robinson, 46th Punjabis, with 2 Indian officers and 204 other ranks of the 91st Punjabis ; against these additions must be set the temporary loss of the services of Captain C. H. Elliott of the Regiment, who was wounded by a stray shot when returning from trench duty.

On December 18th the Commander-in-Chief had ordered the IInd, IIIrd and IVth and Indian Corps to " attack vigorously all along the front," and this led to a certain amount of fighting. On the morning of that date the 58th Rifles, then at Rue de l'Epinette, were ordered to move to a position west of La Quinque Rue to support the Seaforth Highlanders and 2nd Bn. 2nd Gurkhas of the Dehra Dun Brigade ; and during the next forty hours the Regiment was engaged in filling up a gap between these two corps, caused by the Gurkhas having been bombed and shelled out of their trenches. Very heavy fighting ensued, but the 58th more than held its own and succeeded in regaining portions of the lost trenches and in preventing any break-through by the enemy.

The Seaforth Highlanders were very appreciative of the support afforded.

These operations over, the Regiment went back, first to reserve at Richebourg St. Vaast, and then to Fontaines-les-Hermans, where it remained, enjoying a well-earned rest, until January 25th, 1915. During this month the following officers joined, *viz.*, Captains J. J. Tancred,

19th Punjabis, E. Grose, 16th Rajputs, C. G. V. M. Wardell, 21st Punjabis, and Lieutenant S. A. MacMillan, I.A.R.O. Later, on February 12th, a further reinforcement arrived, consisting of 4 Indian officers and 204 other ranks of the 82nd Punjabis, under command of Major J. W. Milne, but as the majority of these either arrived suffering from mumps, or contracted that complaint later, their services were not immediately available.

During the opening two and a half months of the year 1915 the Regiment was not called upon to take part in operations of any outstanding importance; but on March 10th the Battle of Neuve Chapelle commenced, the avowed objects of which were to take some pressure off the Russians, to drive back the, apparently, weakened forces in our front, and to foster the offensive spirit considered likely to have become impaired by the trying experiences of the past winter.

The Indian Corps was now holding the line from the west of Neuve Chapelle to Givenchy, and on the morning of March 9th the Meerut Division was thus disposed :—the Dehra Dun Brigade at La Couture, and the Garhwal Brigade at Richebourg St. Vaast, while the Bareilly Brigade was holding the front line, and was to remain in this position when the two remaining brigades of the Division passed through to the attack. The Regiment was consequently not called upon to take a prominent part in the operations of the four days that the battle lasted, but the trenches occupied were shelled more or less heavily throughout. On the 12th the enemy made a half-hearted attack on the Regiment's front in very misty weather, and a certain number of casualties were incurred—11 Indian ranks being killed; Captains Smith, Grose and Wardell, 1 Indian officer and 24 non-commissioned officers and men being wounded.

The action over, the 58th Rifles marched back to billets in Paradis, and until the beginning of May, when what is known as the Battle of Aubers Ridge opened, the Regiment "carried on" with the ordinary duties of trench warfare. During these weeks reinforcements continued to arrive in parties of varying strength; these, in order of their coming, may be enumerated as follows :—Lieutenant F. H. de V. Robertson, I.A.R.O. and 17 Indian ranks; Major G. J. Davis, 22nd Punjabis, who, however, left in a very few days; 1 Indian officer and 62 other ranks of the 54th Sikhs; 1 Indian officer and 31 other ranks of the 82nd Punjabis; Captain E. C. Creasy, Special Reserve, and Lieutenant C. M. Longbotham, 72nd Punjabis. Against these reinforcements must, however, be set two serious losses—Captain Tancred being seriously wounded on April 25th, while two days later Captain C. H. Elliot, who had only rejoined a week on recovery from his previous wound, was killed by the accidental explosion of a rifle grenade.

On May 4th H.R.H. The Prince of Wales paid a surprise visit to and spent an hour with the Regiment, being introduced and speaking to several Indian officers and appearing to be much interested in all he heard and saw.

The continuous fighting which began on May 9th and continued until the 22nd was undertaken with the double object of supporting the French offensive towards Lens, and of wresting from the enemy Aubers Ridge, the possession of which would menace Lille, Tourcoing, Roubaix and La Bassée. The initial objective of the Indian Corps, on the left of the Ist Corps, was the Ferme du Biez, thereafter the occupation of Ligny-le-Petit, Ligny-le-Grand, the Bois du Biez and La Cliqueterie; the attack was to be carried out by the Meerut Division with the Dehra Dun Brigade in front, the Bareilly Brigade in support and the Garhwal Brigade in reserve, the front of attack being about 650 yards.

At the appointed hour on the 9th the attack was launched, but one assault after another made by the Dehra Dun Brigade failed under the very heavy fire of the enemy, and the Bareilly Brigade was then ordered up in support. In moving forward No. 3 Company of the 58th Rifles came under a very heavy shell fire and had Lieutenant MacMillan mortally wounded, Subadar Bostan Khan and Jemadar Lal Khan killed and 45 casualties among the other ranks.

It was now notified that the Bareilly Brigade would make a fresh attack at 4 p.m. after a further bombardment, and Nos. 1 and 4 Companies of the 58th occupied a portion of the trenches with the Black Watch on the right and the 41st Dogras on the left, the remaining two companies being in support in rear. At 3.50 these front companies went over the parapet and advanced under a very heavy fire, receiving scanty assistance from our own guns which were firing very short; and eventually the line was brought to a stand at a ditch over four and a half feet deep and some ten feet broad. About 5 p.m. it was realized that the attack was hopeless, it having failed of achievement all along the line—the task was impossible, though the attempt was well described by General Willcocks as " one of disciplined valour."

When, at 10.30 p.m., the Regiment was relieved and moved back to dug-outs in Forrester Lane, its losses numbered 2 Indian officers and 38 other ranks killed, 2 British officers—Major Thomson and Captain Bull—5 Indian officers and 197 Indian ranks wounded.

The period from now on to May 19th is remembered as probably the worst and most trying that the 58th Rifles experienced during the whole war. It was throughout under incessant and accurate gun-fire; continuous work was needed to keep the parapets in ordinary repair, and with the constant expectation of counter-attack the nerves of all ranks were under great tension. The losses were very heavy during these days—1 Indian officer and 5 men were killed, 4 Indian officers and 58 men wounded, while Captain F. F. Hodgson died of wounds. By now most of the best of the original manhood of the Regiment were killed and wounded; the reinforcements, largely made up of old and unfit reservists, were unequal to the strain of this kind of warfare, and many of the men sent out were returned to the base as soon as they joined.

No event of special military importance relieved the ordinary routine of trench warfare during the months of June, July and August, while preparations were being made for the autumn offensive at Loos; reinforcements reached the Regiment, 4 British officers—Captains K. B. Mackenzie, J. H. Henderson and A. Flagg, and 2nd-Lieutenant C. M. Durnford—4 Indian officers and 162 other ranks of the 123rd Rifles, and on September 18th the strength and distribution of the 58th were as given in the following table :—

	British Officers.	Indian Officers.	Indian Other Ranks.
Trench Strength	10	15	562
Advanced Depot	1	1	33
Brigade Area	1	1	94
Divisional Area	—	—	16
Elsewhere	—	—	17
Total ...	12	17	722

On September 20th the Bareilly Brigade was inspected by Lord Kitchener.

The work allotted to the Indian Corps in the operations projected for the latter part of September, 1915, was to seize Aubers Ridge and then, advancing south-east, to turn the defences of La Bassée from the north; and the attack was to be made on the 25th by the Meerut Division, the Bareilly Brigade on the left, the Garhwal on the right and the Dehra Dun Brigade in reserve, each brigade having three battalions in the front line and two in reserve.* In the Bareilly Brigade the 2nd and 1/4th Black Watch and 69th Punjabis were in the front line, the 33rd Punjabis and the 58th Rifles in reserve, the last named being in the Rue Tilleloy.

At about 5.50 a.m. on September 25th the front line advanced to the attack, the 58th then moving forward and occupying the trenches vacated by the 2nd Black Watch. At 6.15 Nos. 2 and 4 Companies crossed the parapet, advanced some 400 yards and then "dug in," when the remaining two companies came up, went through Nos. 2 and 4, reached the German second line and began to consolidate. But here it became apparent that the attack by the brigade on the right had not made sufficient ground to allow of the Bareilly Brigade unduly exposing its right.

At 10.30 a.m. the left of the Brigade became equally uncovered, and the enemy, quick to notice this, now heavily attacked this flank, when the line began to give way. Gallant efforts were made to hold up the enemy, especially by No. 2 Company under Subadar Tikka Khan, but the German attack had been admirably organized and was vigorously pushed, and by noon there was nothing to be done but to retire to the original line in as good order as possible. Here the Regiment was relieved at six on the following morning, and marched back to billets at Pont du Hem under 2nd-Lieutenant Durnford, the only British officer left of those who had gone into action with the Regiment, which had lost 8 British officers, 6 Indian officers and 246 other ranks, killed, wounded and missing. Among the killed was the Commanding Officer, Lieut.-Colonel Davidson-Houston, a great loss to the Regiment,

* The Indian Corps brigades now contained each two British battalions—one Regular and one Territorial—and three Indian.

to which he was devoted and in which practically all his service had been passed. Of the other British officers, Captain Flagg, Lieutenants Milligan and Nicolls were killed, Captains Wardell, Mackenzie and Harcourt wounded, and Lieutenant Deane-Spread was missing.

Captain Pope now rejoined from duty with the Divisional Signals Company and assumed temporary command of the Regiment, until relieved a few days later by Captain Lind at Gorre, where Captain Willis and 2nd-Lieutenant A. J. O'Connor, I.A.R.O., also joined for duty.

During the Givenchy operations early in October the Regiment was not actively engaged, but the trenches occupied were subjected to some shelling, and 2nd-Lieutenant O'Connor and a number of men were wounded.

The Regiment was now withdrawn from the front and re-organized. Lieut.-Colonel F. R. B. Murray, 90th Punjabis, joined and assumed command; Captain H. J. Davson, 82nd Punjabis, Lieutenants G. C. Bampfield, 90th Punjabis, R. J. K. Todd, 93rd Burmah Infantry, and A. Saunders, I.A.R.O., also joined, while the return of men from hospital or the base and the arrival of drafts from the 54th, 66th, 76th, 82nd and 123rd Regiments, brought the strength up to 10 British officers, 9 Indian officers and 575 Indian other ranks.

The last tour of duty of the 58th in the trenches in France ended on October 29th, and on the 31st information was received that the Indian Corps would shortly be required to embark at Marseilles for service in another theatre of war. On November 30th the Regiment marched to Lillers and entrained, arriving at Marseilles on December 3rd, and there embarking in the ss. *Ivernia* on the 6th in company with the 33rd Punjabis and two companies of Sappers, the headquarters of the Division and of the Bareilly and Dehra Dun Brigades.

The Battalion embarked at a strength of 10 British officers, 21 Indian officers and 799 other ranks.

Disembarking at Port Said on December 14th, the Regiment was sent at once by train to camp at Suez where it remained until the 27th, and thereafter had many moves from one place to another. It proceeded first to El Shatt on the east bank of the Suez Canal, moved thence on January 23rd, 1916, to Gebel Murr, a low hill some seven miles east of Suez, went back again to El Shatt on February 8th, and three days later was sent to Ajun Musa, five miles south-east of Suez on the east bank of the Canal, the position here being a low, sandy ridge about 2,000 yards in length running from north to south.

During these days much had happened in the way of reconstruction; the headquarter staff of the Lahore and Meerut Divisions, the brigade staffs and some of the original units of those formations had gone to Mesopotamia, other regiments were sent to East Africa, some to India and one or two to Aden; but the majority of the infantry battalions were ordered to remain in Egypt—the 58th Rifles among the number—and this was at first attached to the 31st Indian Infantry Brigade, but early in February was definitely posted to the 20th Indian Infantry Brigade, commanded by Brigadier-General H. D. Watson, C.M.G., C.I.E., M.V.O., and containing also the 2nd Bn. 3rd Gurkhas, the Alwar and the Gwalior Infantry; the Brigade was attached to the 54th East Anglian Division under Major-General S. W. Hare, C.B.

By this time many of the attached units from other corps had left the 58th either to rejoin their own regiments or to reinforce others. Thus, on January 8th 3 British officers, 3 Indian officers and 184 other ranks of the 123rd Rifles left to reinforce the 104th; on the 25th 6 Indian officers and 251 non-commissioned officers and men of the 54th Sikhs and 82nd Punjabis were taken away to join the 53rd Sikhs and 82nd Punjabis respectively; and between January 1st and the 18th these losses were to some extent made good by the arrival of two British officers—2nd-Lieutenants A. I. G. McConkey (Unattached List) and G. G. Hills, I.A.R.O.—2 Indian officers and 120 rank and file from Marseilles, 54 non-commissioned officers and men from the Depot in India, and 1 Indian officer and 15 other ranks from hospital in England.

During March and April further reinforcements arrived, and by the middle of the latter month the strength of the Regiment stood at 12 British officers, 19 Indian officers and 735 other ranks.

During the whole of the rest of the year the Regiment was fully occupied in reorganization, training, and work upon the defences of the Suez Canal, in the making of roads and laying of light railways and pipe-lines, without which these defences could not be occupied. Reinforcements arrived from time to time and British officers came and went; reconnaissances were occasionally sent forward towards the passes connecting Sinai with the Suez Canal plain east of Bir Mabeuik, and once or twice shots at long range were exchanged with enemy vedettes; but the work demanded of the troops was very monotonous and unexciting, and all were relieved and grateful when, at the end of September, furlough to India was opened to the Indian ranks.

On August 23rd the Sikh Company of the Regiment had been sent to Somaliland under Major R. de W. Waller and Lieutenant G. R. Dowland, and at the close of this month the distribution of the 58th Rifles was as under :—

	British Officers.	Indian Officers.	Indian Other Ranks.
At Ajun Musa	8	5	250
At Bir Mabeuik	8	5	306
Gone to Somaliland ...	2	5	188

But in December the Regiment was ordered to relieve the 2nd Bn. 3rd Gurkhas in two posts known as Abu Zanima and Tor, situated on the east coast of the Gulf of Suez and respectively sixty and 120 miles to the east of that port. On the 18th of this month the 58th embarked at Port Tewfiq in the ss. *Georgian*, and two days later 3 British and 4 Indian officers with 306 other ranks under Major Lind were landed at, and took over, the post of Abu Zanima, the transport then going on to Tor where the remainder of the Regiment was put ashore and took over on the 22nd from the 2nd Bn. 3rd Gurkhas. These posts were held by the Regiment until August and September, 1917, respectively, though the strength of the garrisons was later considerably reduced, in February, 1917, all the 58th Rifles, except one company at each post, being recalled to the neighbourhood of the Suez Canal.

The 58th Rifles now formed part of the 29th Indian Infantry Brigade, and was engaged soon after return to Egypt in operations described as under in the Official History :—*" The Turks were emboldened to re-occupy Nekhl and Bir-el-Hassana with small detachments. On February 18th three columns were dispatched against

* "Official History of the War: Egypt and Palestine," Vol. I, p. 277.

these posts. That against Bir-el-Hassana marched from El Arish, and consisted of the 2nd Bn. Imperial Camel Corps and one section of the Hong-Kong Battery. The small garrison of Hassana was surprised, 3 officers and 19 other ranks, with a quantity of stores, being captured. The two columns marching on Nekhl came from the Canal, the northern, from Serapeum, consisting of the 11th A. L. H., the southern, from Suez, of the headquarters 6th Mounted Brigade, detachments of Yeomanry of that brigade and the 58th Rifles. The enemy garrison at Nekhl, composed of about 100 cavalry, was warned by Bedouin of the British advance and fell back towards Aqaba, leaving a field gun and 11 prisoners in British hands."

At the end of April the Regiment was sent to a segregation camp near El Shatt, as there was some bubonic plague among troops of other corps, and remained here until June 25th, but it was not affected by plague. During this time a good deal of useful training was carried out and the Sikh Company rejoined from Somaliland. The Regiment, now five companies strong, moved to Ismailia and was reorganized as under by Major A. G. Lind :—

"A" Company, Captain R. B. Kitson, 2 platoons Dogras, 2 platoons Yusafzais.

"B" Company, Lieutenant G. R. Dowland, 4 platoons Punjabi Mahammedans.

"C" Company, Major R. de W. Waller, 4 platoons Sikhs.

"D" Company, Lieutenant E. G. Ekin, 1 platoon Punjabi Mahammedans of 55th, 1 platoon Afridis, 1 platoon Khattaks 1 platoon Yusafzais, both of these last of the 55th (Coke's) Rifles F.F.

On September 2nd the detachments rejoined and the 58th Rifles was now under orders to proceed to the Palestine front to join the 234th Brigade of a Division, the 75th, which had recently been organized, taking the place in the Brigade of a battalion which was decimated with fever contracted in East Africa.

On June 28th General Sir E. Allenby had assumed command of the Egyptian Expeditionary Force in succession to General Sir A. Murray, and the enemy now held a strong position some thirty miles in length extending from the sea at Gaza to Beersheba. "I had decided," wrote General Allenby*, "to strike the main blow against the left flank of the main Turkish position, Hareira and Sheria. The capture of Beersheba was a necessary preliminary to this operation, in order to secure the water supplies at that place and to give room for the deployment of the attacking force on the high ground to the north and north-west of Beersheba, from which direction I intended to attack the Hareira-Sheria line."

The 75th Division was commanded by Major-General P. C. Palin, C.B., C.M.G., and the 234th Infantry Brigade was made up of the 1st Bn. 4th Duke of Cornwall's Light Infantry, 2nd Bn. 4th Dorsetshire Regiment, the 58th Vaughan's Rifles (F.F.) and the 123rd Outram's Rifles; its commander was Brigadier-General F. J. Anley, C.B., C.M.G. During the month of October the 75th Division was concentrated in the Mansura area.

In the attack upon and capture of Beersheba on October 31st, the 75th Division was not immediately concerned, these operations being entrusted to troops of the 53rd, 60th and 74th Divisions, nor was it engaged in the attack on Gaza; but the trenches occupied by the 58th Rifles during these days were under constant enemy shell fire, and several casualties were incurred. On Gaza falling, however, the 75th Division moved forward and by November 12th had advanced about thirty miles north of Gaza, and now had the Anzac Mounted Division on its right and the 52nd Division on its left; while the Turks, immediately opposed by the 232nd and 233rd Brigades of the 75th Division—the 234th Brigade being in reserve—were holding a strong line of defence behind the villages of Yasur, El Kustineh and Tel El Turmis. The Division was now directed to push back the enemy, to advance at all costs and capture the Junction railway station some eight miles further north, where the lines of rail from Jerusalem and Ramleh met. The capture of this junction—the third of the three objectives entrusted to the Division—was to be the work of the 234th Brigade.

The attack commenced at 9.30 a.m. on the 13th and met with a stout resistance, and, the right flank of the Brigade becoming

* Despatch of December 16th, 1917.

somewhat exposed during the advance, "D" Company of the Regiment under Captain Kitson was detached to protect this flank; the ground passed over was very much broken and this company got out of sight and touch and became engaged with a considerable body of the enemy. Captain Kitson, apprehensive of counter-attack, appears to have ordered "D" Company to extend and attack. In so doing the company suffered heavy loss, Captain Kitson, Lieutenant Douglas and 23 other ranks being killed, while 3 of the 4 Indian officers and 43 men were wounded; but there can be no doubt that the action of this company checked a very strong counter-attack which the Turks were about to launch.

The Brigade meanwhile was continuing to advance, and by 11 p.m., had arrived about a mile and a half to the west of the Junction, where the enemy was met and hurriedly fell back. Here the Brigade entrenched for the night, and on again advancing in the morning found that the position was vacated and the enemy in full retreat, leaving only a rearguard to cover his retirement. Many prisoners were here taken.

The Brigade remained more or less in this position until the evening of the 18th, when orders were received that the 75th Division was to advance with the City of Jerusalem as its objective; while to the 58th Rifles a special mission was assigned—to picquet the pass north-east of Latrun, the Regiment being temporarily attached to the 223rd Brigade, which it was to join on the morning of November 19th at Latrun.

Moving off, after many delays, the Regiment arrived at Latrun at 10 a.m., and at the actual pass some hour and a half later, greeted here by a few enemy shells. The Regiment was now informed that very few of the enemy were to be seen and that but slight opposition need be expected; but almost directly the picqueting of the pass commenced, the enemy showed in strength and put up everywhere a stout resistance, and in the event Major Waller and thirty-four men were wounded and six were killed. The Regiment remained in charge of the pass for many hours and was then sent on to hold the village of Saba, while the Brigade, with the 233rd, went on to the capture of Nebi Samwil, the key-position of Jerusalem, and was not relieved—after suffering much discomfort from cold, rain, half-rations, etc.—until November 24th, when it was recalled to its own Brigade and marched to Kuriya-el-Enab, finally going into camp at Beshitt on the 27th to rest and refit.

During this month the 58th Rifles had suffered the following casualties :—2 British officers, 1 Indian officer and 36 other ranks killed ; 1 British officer, 4 Indian officers and 95 Indian non-commissioned officers and men wounded.

When on December 9th our troops entered Jerusalem, Subadar-Major Tikka Khan was detailed with fifty men to take over charge of the Mahammedan holy places in the city.

The 58th Rifles now, on December 10th, received orders to join the 232nd Brigade then at Jimsu, where it arrived the same day after a march across a roadless, rain-sodden country, and on the 11th "the 75th Division advanced its front to the line Midieh—Kh. Hamid—Budrus—Sheik Obeid Rahil in the XXIst Corps area, meeting with slight opposition in the process. An enemy counter-attack, after a preliminary bombardment of the Zeifizfiyeh Ridge was repulsed."* On this day "C" Company under Major A. A. Smith—who had only rejoined a few days previously from command of the regimental depot at Multan—supported a company of the 4th Devons in the capture of the Khurbat Zebdah Ridge, then passing through and taking Khurbat Hamid, after a short fight in which one man was killed and two wounded. At the same time "A" Company, under Lieutenant E. G. Ekin, assisted the 2/3rd Gurkhas in the capture of Budras village, putting an enemy machine gun out of action and making prisoners of a Turkish officer and ten men.

On December 15th the Regiment was on the left of the Brigade in the storming of the very steep Khurbat Ibanneh position, taking prisoners 2 officers and 11 men ; the casualties in the 58th from the 1st to the 31st were 4 men killed and 18 wounded, while the captures totalled 3 officers, 25 men and one machine gun.

From this time until January 11th, 1918, the 58th Rifles were at Beit Nabala in reserve to the 233rd Brigade ; for a week after this the Regiment was at Haditheh in divisional reserve ; and finally on January

* "The Advance of the Egyptian Expeditionary Force," p. 178.

18th it moved to a camp near Ludd where it came into corps reserve. During nearly the whole of this time it was engaged in road-making, most of the time in exceedingly wet weather and with only waterproof sheets as shelters, but reinforcements had continued to arrive, and early in February the Regiment stood at a strength of 13 British officers, 18 Indian officers and 1,058 other ranks, while 7 British signallers and 27 Indian drivers were attached for duty.

Rumours of a forward move had for some time past been in circulation, but it was not until March 10th that the Regiment rejoined the 234th Brigade, Headquarters and half the Regiment going to Bireh, while the other wing under Major Smith was sent to Et Tireh. The advance was to begin on the 12th and the rôle assigned to the 58th Rifles was the construction and improvement of communications in rear of the advanced troops to facilitate the rapid passage of guns and supplies.

The XXth and XXIst Corps, to the latter of which the 75th Division belonged, were now to advance on a front of twenty-six miles from Kefr Malik to El Mirr, and of an average depth of seven miles.

The advance duly commenced on the date appointed, the Turkish front being penetrated to a depth of three and a half miles on a front of three miles, and the Regiment did good work in road construction and final consolidation in very difficult country. On March 18th the 58th was placed again in the front line, joining the 233rd Brigade* at Abud ; and on the same night the wing under Major Smith advanced upon and captured, with but small opposition, the village of Deir Gussaneh and the Sheikh Kauwash Ridge, the other wing following in close support. The Regiment was now on the extreme right flank of the Division, connecting on the left with the 2nd Bn. 3rd Gurkhas and on the right with the left battalion of the 10th Division.

To the left front of the ridge now occupied, and on the front slope of a lower ridge, was the strongly-built village of El Kefr, occupied by Turks with machine guns ; and a strong patrol sent out from the 58th Rifles on the 22nd found the village well defended and met with a good

* It will be seen that the Regiment did not definitely belong to any particular brigade, but was something of a " surplus " battalion in the 75th Division.

deal of resistance, having two men killed and seven wounded. A few nights later a hill commanding El Kefr village—but itself commanded by a ridge some 500 yards distant—was occupied by " C " Company under Major Waller and Captain Gillespie, and held against heavy fire and some rather feeble enemy attacks; and then on March 29th verbal orders were received that the 58th Rifles were to capture and hold El Kefr village, which also entailed the capture of Sheikh Nafukh Ridge, for unless this were in our possession the village could not be held.

It was decided that the position should be approached during the night and the assault pushed in at dawn.

It was arranged that two platoons of a company of a Deccan Regiment, lately attached to the 58th, should seize the Sheikh Nafukh Ridge and secure the right, sending up a green Véry light when this had been done; upon which two platoons from another company of the Regiment, which by then would be occupying the re-entrant from the Wadi Ballut to El Kefr village, were to push forward and, assisted by another two platoons already on El Kefr Hill, assault the village, the other platoons securing the left flank and covering the retirement should the attack fail. At 4.45 a.m. on March 30th the two Deccani platoons had gained their objective without opposition and sent up the signal agreed upon, when the centre attack was loosed. Half an hour later a very heavy fire broke out from El Kefr village and Sheikh Nafukh Hill, and it was now learnt from Lieutenant Hills, who was in command on El Kefr Hill, that one of his platoons and the two others from the Wadi Ballut direction, had attacked as arranged, but that a very heavy fire had been met, his platoon was practically out of action, and that, though the other two had reached and penetrated the village, they had then been assailed from the right and were unable to extricate themselves. It was now apparent that the right had never been secured, and, when the enemy attacked, these platoons almost at once fell back, thus exposing the remainder of the attacking party to the fire and counter-attacks of the defenders of the ridge and village.

Reinforcements were sent up from the 58th and other regiments of the Brigade and the hill was held; later it took a full battalion of infantry, supported by the fire of heavy howitzers, to capture the ridge and village—a task entrusted on this occasion to five platoons and a field battery. The losses in these five platoons were heavy—Lieutenant J. McKay and 12 Indian other ranks being killed, Captain D. Montford and 34 men were missing—most of these killed—while 68 men were wounded.

The enemy maintained a heavy fire and made several attacks upon the position during the next few days, the village and ridge being held, although with some difficulty, until the success of operations further to the east relieved the pressure ; the Regiment had two more men killed and two wounded, and the total loss from March 22nd to the 31st amounted to 2 British officers, 1 Indian officer and 20 other ranks killed, 1 Indian officer and 80 other ranks wounded, leaving the 58th Rifles at a strength of 11 British officers, 12 Indian officers and 829 non-commissioned officers and men.

In the initial operations connected with the capture of El Kefr and Berukin villages and the intervening ridge of Sheikh Nafukh the Regiment was not actively engaged. It was, however, called up later, and between April 9th and 12th had seven men killed, Lieutenant S. T. Gray and 63 Indian ranks wounded and 3 men missing.

Preparations had been made for continuing the advance, but these were cancelled and orders issued to take up a strong defensive line, this policy being dictated by the course of recent events on the Western Front, and by the fact that the many units sent from Palestine to France during the period of emergency had not yet been replaced.

From April 27th to May 7th the 58th Rifles occupied the Rafat salient, and either here or in reserve at Rentis it remained until the night of August 30th and 31st, when—the 75th Division having been continuously in the line since April—it was relieved by the troops of the 10th Division and by the French Palestine Detachment ; it then moved back to Beit Nabala and thence to Mulebbis, where an extensive system of training, over ground similar to the enemy positions, was undergone in preparation for a fresh " push " believed now to be imminent.

The XXIst Corps, containing the 3rd (Lahore), 7th (Meerut), 54th, 60th and 75th Divisions, with an Australian cavalry brigade, two brigades of mountain artillery and eighteen batteries of heavy and siege guns, was to attack the Turkish defences in the coastal area, break through between the railway and the sea and seize the foothills south-east of Jiljulieh. It was then to swing to the right on the line Hableh—Tul Keram, and advance in a north-easterly direction through the hills, converging on Samaria and Attara, so as to drive the enemy up the Messudieh—Jenin Road, into the arms of the cavalry at El Afule.*

In the attack by the 75th Division, commencing at 4.30 a.m. on September 19th, on the strongly-held Tabsor defences, it was directed that the 232nd and 234th Brigades would be in the front line on the right and left respectively, the 234th Brigade covering a front of 1,000 yards with the 58th Rifles on the left and the 1st Bn. 152nd Indian Infantry on the right. The 58th, moving off on a front of 400 yards only, was to capture the village of Tabsor and the defence system of 500 yards to the east of it, thereafter gradually extending as it moved on, until on arrival at the final objective, 8,000 yards distant, it would be covering a front of nearly 1,000 yards.

The Regiment advanced in two waves at 150 yards interval, "A" Company (Captain Ekin) on the left and "B" (Lieutenant Bradford) on the right of the first wave, and "C" (Captain Gillespie) and "D" Company (Lieutenant Dunn) on left and right respectively of the second. Covered by an intense bombardment from our guns the line advanced, and came three minutes later under the enemy counter-barrage which fell heavily on the second wave. The Turkish front line of defence was taken with but trifling opposition at 4.47, Tabsor village was encircled, its defenders flying in a westerly direction, and at 5.26 the enemy second line was reached, where, "according to plan," a ten-minutes' halt was called for reorganization and readjustment of direction.

The final objective was gained by 8 a.m. and the 75th Division was here halted and passed into corps reserve, and so ended for the 58th Vaughan's Rifles any further share in the operations of the Palestine campaign.

On this day the Regiment was opposed to the 61st Regiment of the 20th Turkish Division, said to be one of the "crack" corps of the Osmanli Army, and from this the 58th captured a hundred prisoners, six machine guns, two .77 millimetre guns and a 5.9 howitzer ; while the

* General Allenby's despatch of October 31st, 1918.

casualties—chiefly caused by the enemy counter-barrage—amounted to 7 Indian ranks killed, 2nd-Lieutenant A. H. C. Allen, Subadar Mahammed Arbi, I.O.M., 2 British and 37 Indian other ranks wounded.

At midnight on this day the Division was concentrated about Et Tireh and Miskeh, and here the Regiment remained some ten days engaged in salvage work, interrupted by a severe epidemic of Spanish influenza which now broke out, and which sent many of all ranks to hospital.

On October 31st, while at Kirkuk, the welcome news was received of the conclusion of an armistice with the Turks, followed on November 4th by the announcement of the surrender of Austria, and on the 11th by the news that an armistice had been concluded with our arch-enemy Germany.

On November 18th the 58th moved to Sarona, near Jaffa, on December 3rd to Ludd, where two days later it entrained in two parties—total strength 22 British officers, 14 Indian officers, 33 British and 596 Indian other ranks—for the infantry base at Kantara, where it went into camp on the Kantara—El Arish road, remaining here until March 17th, 1919, on that date proceeding to Suez, ostensibly in view of an early return to India.

These agreeable anticipations were not, however, realized, for in March there were serious risings in Egypt against Europeans, many of whom were murdered in Upper Egypt, and orders were received to take all possible precautions and mount guards over railway stations, docks and all important public buildings ; while further reports coming in as to the state of unrest in the Egyptian army and police, it quickly became known that no troops could be permitted to leave the country until quiet had been thoroughly restored.

From April 15th to May 5th the Regiment was quartered at Abbasia near Cairo, and on this latter date it was ordered at short notice to Minia, a large town in Upper Egypt, and from there to take over garrison duty at Beni Mazar, a small place some thirty miles to the north ; as a result, Headquarters and " B " and " D " Companies were sent to Minia, while " A " and " C " under Captain Gillespie moved to Beni Mazar, two platoons also, commanded by Lieutenant

Fagarty, going to Kerkas, twelve miles south of Minia. The 58th was now in the 10th Division of the Army of Occupation.

There had been a good deal of disaffection in Minia prior to the arrival of the Regiment, but during the five months that it garrisoned that place and Beni Mazar there was no trouble with the people of either town.

In July the following proceeded to England to represent the Regiment at the peace celebrations in London :—Acting Subadar-Major Indar Singh, M.C., I.D.S.M., Acting Havildar-Major Mir Mahammed and Lance-Naik Kapura, the first-named of these receiving his Military Cross from the hands of His Majesty the King-Emperor.

On September 25th the Regiment moved to Dumanhour, some twenty miles south of Alexandria and near Tanta, and like the latter a somewhat seditious centre ; and in November and December there were signs of unrest. Displays of force, however, kept the disaffected under some degree of restraint and no serious trouble resulted.

On January 24th, 1920, a warning order to embark for India was received ; this was confirmed on the 27th, when definite orders were given to entrain on the 29th. On this day detachments from the Guides Infantry and the 2nd Bn. 56th Punjab Rifles arrived and took over the garrison duties, and, entraining that evening, the Regiment reached Suez and at once embarked in the transport *Franz Ferdinand,* the strength being 7 British and 12 Indian officers and 736 other ranks with 21 followers. The following British officers embarked :—Lieut.-Colonel A. G. Lind, D.S.O., Captains A. I. G. McConkey, R. G. Ekin and E. M. Ashton, Lieutenants C. R. Spear, M. B. P. Reeve and T. L. Evans.

As the 47th Sikhs were accommodated in the same ship there were more than 1,450 troops on board, and the men were much crowded.

Karachi was reached on February 9th, and next day the Regiment disembarked and proceeded to the rest camp, occupying the same lines as five and a half years previously when on its way to France.

On the 13th the 58th Rifles entrained and arrived at Multan on the 14th, where on landing it was played to the lines occupied by the Depot by the bands of the Buffs and 14th Sikhs, and the next two days were devoted to feasting and *tamasha.*

SURVIVORS OF 1914-15. THAL, 1926

BRITISH AND INDIAN OFFICERS, PAST AND PRESENT. THAL, 1926

CHAPTER IV.

Fourth Period. 1920—1926.

It was notified in the *Gazette of India*, under No. 845, of June, 1920, that Subadar Gujar Singh had been awarded the Second Class of the Order of British India, in recognition of conspicuously good service rendered in India during the Great War of 1914-18. This Indian officer was at the time serving in Waziristan with the 57th Rifles, Frontier Force, to which regiment a draft of 120 men had been sent from the Depot of the 58th in May of the year previous. That regiment had done very good service on the march to Thal and the Kurram, when the army of Afghanistan was besieging the former place, and later in the heavy fighting with the Mahsud Wazirs in the Takki Zam in 1919-20. Subadar Gujar Singh had been appointed Officiating Subadar-Major of the 57th Rifles, but on the departure to pension of Subadar-Major Tikka Khan, Subadar Gujar Singh rejoined his own corps, of which he was then appointed Subadar-Major.

Something should now be said as to actual happenings on the North-West Frontier immediately prior to the return to India of the 58th Rifles, and as to the state of affairs on the Border in the early months of 1920.

" After many years of peace there was a recrudescence of trouble in Afghanistan and all along the border between that country and India. On February 22nd the Ameer Habib Ullah Khan, who had always been a loyal friend to Great Britain, was murdered whilst camping in the Laghman Valley. . . . The new Ameer, Aman Ullah, began his reign by announcing that he would punish those who were guilty of the assassination of his father, that he would institute reforms in the country, and that he would preserve the tradition of friendship with India. . . . Possibly, owing to the intrigues of the Russian Government, the new Ameer did not long keep his promise of preserving friendship with Great Britain. Early in May, 1919, a large Afghan army came pouring across the frontier and proceeded to pillage far and wide in the north-west provinces. The act of war seems to have been somewhat unofficial, however, for within a few days, and before the Afghans had suffered any serious defeats, the Ameer entered into tentative negotiations with the Indian Government. The fighting continued, however, . . . The aeroplanes attached to the Anglo-Indian forces bombed both Jellalabad and Kabul. After much procrastination a peace conference was opened at Rawal Pindi on July 26th. . . . A preliminary peace was signed on August 8th."*

During these troubles certain of the tribes of Waziristan made common cause with the Afghans, but at the time the Government of India had not found it convenient to punish them in the manner deserved. In November of this year, however, the Afghan menace being checked, both the Tochi Wazirs and the Mahsuds were summoned to attend meetings to hear the terms which the Government intended to impose upon them; and in the event of these terms not being accepted it was proposed to deal first with the Wazirs and later with the Mahsuds, a force of close upon 30,000 men being detailed for any operations which might become necessary. The offending tribesmen refused to agree to the terms offered them, and operations consequently took place, these lasting from November, 1919, until May, 1920, by which time, in the words of the Official Account,† it had been realized that "it was impossible to force this tribe" (the Mahsuds) "of unruly and obdurate individuals, recognizing no responsible leaders and no form of organized government, to make any engagements, or to keep such promises if made, once the troops had left the country."

A change of policy was now adopted; active operations were for the present to be in abeyance, but the troops were to remain in the country, while roads suitable for mechanical transport were henceforth to be constructed to facilitate its occupation. Certain of the regiments employed were sent back to India, but the Waziristan Force remained in being, brigades being maintained at Tank, Sorarogha, Ladha and Piazha Raghza with additional troops on the lines of communication.

In May the 58th Rifles received orders to prepare to move to

* Annual Register for 1919, pp. 255, 256.

† "Operations in Waziristan, 1919-20," pp. 142, 143.

Waziristan, and on June 10th it entrained at Multan for Mari Indus, leaving behind a Depot under the command of Captain D. S. Gillespie. Tank was reached on the 12th from where the Regiment marched to Kotkai in the Takki Zam, and from there to Sorarogha, joining here the 43rd Infantry Brigade. The Regiment was at this time very weak in all ranks, containing only 6 British officers, 7 Indian officers and 425 Indian other ranks, for a number of Indian officers and men were away on special war furlough, while a great many men had recently been demobilized. Of those now composing the Regiment, the newly-promoted Indian officers and non-commissioned officers had had but little time or opportunity for training, and nothing of the nature of "mountain warfare" had been practised since the Regiment had picquetted the Latrun Pass for the 233rd Brigade during the advance on Jerusalem in 1917. However, the good tradition and sound methods of the 58th, and the natural instinct of the Indian officers and men for the practice of hill warfare, made all ranks keen to prove themselves equal to anything that might be demanded of them, and it was not long before convoy and picquetting duties were being carried out efficiently.

No actual operations were being undertaken against the Mahsuds at the time of the arrival of the Regiment in Waziristan; but several sections of the tribe were actively hostile, and parties of them were always on the look-out to take immediate advantage of any slackness or ignorance of ordinary precautions, and "incidents" were of almost daily occurrence.

In July, 1920, the Regiment moved to Piazha Raghza, where it almost at once began to suffer from malaria, as many as seventy cases appearing on the sick report, and over 100 men having to be sent down the line to the base.

At the same time some little trouble was also experienced over what was known as the "Muhajerin" movement among the Yusafzais—a movement instigated by Mahammedan agitators, who were dissatisfied with the peace terms made by the British Government with that of Turkey. Numbers of Indian Mahammedans left India, many of these going to Amb and to Agror, in the neighbourhood of the Black Mountain, where since 1830 the Hindustani fanatics had made their home, and whence they had time after time carried out propaganda and active intrigues against the Government of India. The Hindustani fanatics at this time were largely instrumental in working on the religious feelings of the Yusafzais, and the families of many men of these tribes, who were serving in Indian regiments, sold their lands and joined in a migratory move into Afghanistan. This led to numbers of men demanding their immediate discharge, and there were some cases of desertion, and even of insubordination which had to be severely dealt with.

In the end the Yusafzais came to realize that they had been egregiously deceived, and very many returned to their country where they were well received and cared for by the local government, which at once took all possible steps to assist them in regaining their properties which they had sold for absurdly small sums to Hindu opportunists and profiteers.

In September the 58th Rifles were moved to Ladha, the furthest post up the line, remaining here until October, in which month it was decided to send a column to reoccupy Wana, which had been deserted since 1919, when the trans-border *personnel* of the South Waziristan Militia mutinied and forced the loyal portion of the corps to retire towards the Zhob Valley. Since then Wana had been looted and burned by the local inhabitants.

The Regiment was detailed to accompany this column and marched on October 28th from Ladha, arriving two days later at Jandola, where the column was concentrating; it was composed of two brigades, the 23rd and 24th, and the whole force was under the command of Major-General W. S. Leslie, C.M.G., D.S.O., and the Regiment was told off to the 24th Indian Infantry Brigade, which contained also the 2nd Bn. Norfolk Regiment, the 4th Bn. 3rd Gurkhas and the 2nd Bn. 41st Dogras; it was commanded by Colonel (Temporary Brigadier-General) O. C. Borrett, C.M.G., D.S.O., A.D.C. The strength of the 58th Rifles was now 14 British officers, 15 Indian officers and 658 rank and file.

The object and scope of the operations in which the Regiment was now to take part are described as follows in General Lord Rawlinson's despatch of October 23rd, 1921 :—

" It had been intended to operate against the Wana Wazirs during the spring of 1920 to punish this tribe for the many outrages it had been guilty of during 1919. During the latter year the Afghans . . . had sent a small detachment to Wana . . . Later the Afghan contingent was strengthened. . . . Throughout the summer the contingent remained in Wazir territory and continued to receive assistance from Afghanistan in money, ammunition and rations. The presence of these Afghan adventurers precluded any real attempt on the part of the Wana Wazirs to approach Government with a view to submission.

"The determined resistance of the Mahsuds rendered an expedition against the Wana Wazirs in the spring of 1920 impossible, and it was postponed, but towards the end of the summer the Government of India decided that operations against the Wana Wazirs should take place in the autumn unless our terms were complied with, and ordered the concentration of the Wana column at Jandola." Certain terms were offered to the Wana Wazirs, who were directed to hand over a moiety of the fines in rifles and money demanded through a fully representative jirga at Murtaza by November 10th ; but the jirga failed to attend, and it appeared that while a considerable body of the tribesmen were willing to make peace, there was a larger party, led by one Haji Abdur Razaq, a notorious anti-British agent, which was against compliance. It was obvious, therefore, that no settlement was likely until the Haji and his followers had been forced to leave the country.

On November 12th, then, the Wana column moved to Chagmalai, one mile to the west of the entrance to the Shahur Tangi, and during the next two days permanent picquets were here erected and occupied. On the 15th the column advanced through the Shahur Tangi to Haidari Kach, the Regiment finding the advanced guard and picquetting troops. There was no really serious opposition beyond that about one mile from Haidari Kach some few of the enemy opened fire from the left flank, but these were quickly turned out of their position by "B" Company.

On the 18th the column moved on to Sarwekai, encountering no opposition *en route*, and the old fort being found to be in possession of Mahsud "friendlies." The 58th remained, however, for the present in occupation of the camp at Haidari Kach and of all the picquets from the western entrance of the Shahur Tangi up to midway to Sarwekai.

At Sarwekai the Wana Wazirs were afforded a further opportunity of reconsidering their attitude before the column made a fresh advance; the friendly sections made overtures for peace and began to bring in instalments of their fines, but the hostile sections stood aloof, and consequently the advance to Wana was ordered to begin on December 16th.

Before this date two officers had joined the Regiment for duty—Captain J. R. Wynter, D.S.O., 52nd Sikhs, Frontier Force, and Lieutenant J. S. Jenkins, 9th Bhopal Infantry, while within the last few days the 23rd Brigade had begun to close up to the front, and on December 12th the 2nd Bn. Royal West Surrey Regiment relieved the 58th Rifles, which moved on and rejoined its own Brigade at Sarwekai.

Two battalions of the 23rd Brigade were now brought up to and remained at Sarwekai, while the remainder of the column marched to Dargai Oba, the 58th again providing the advanced guard. The route chosen was by a path about two miles to the south of the old Militia road and proved to be very bad, the country from the western end of the Sarwekai Plain as far as Dargai Oba being a mass of broken hills and nullahs, very blind country and difficult to picquet. The advanced guard was sniped at rather heavily when commencing the long and steep descent of the Shina Pal Lar to Dargai Oba, but the enemy made nowhere any real stand, and the Regiment was able to occupy the camping ground and put out the necessary picquets with a loss of only three men wounded.

On December 17th the troops were employed in improving a more northerly and better road back towards Sarwekai, and in constructing permanent picquet posts for its protection, and next day the advance was continued to Karab Kot. The Regiment was this day on rear-guard and did not get into camp until 9 p.m., for the advanced guard met with a certain amount of opposition. At Karab Kot orders were issued that the Headquarters and two companies of the Regiment should remain here with one company of the 2nd Bn. 61st Pioneers, and a camp for these companies was selected and entrenched at Rogha Kot, about a mile further on, and this was occupied on the 21st, the remainder of the 58th proceeding next day with the column to Wana which was reached and occupied without opposition.

It had originally been the intention of the officer commanding the column to remain sufficiently long at Wana to enable the column to carry out a number of punitive expeditions in the immediate neighbourhood, to destroy the fort and then withdraw to Jandola; but in view of the fact that a mission had recently been dispatched to Kabul to arrange a treaty with the Afghan Government, it was now considered that it would probably strengthen the hands of the mission if the Wana column remained for the present where it was. No punitive expeditions of any kind were therefore undertaken, and the force remained inactive from the date of the occupation of Wana on December 22nd, 1920, to the end of January, 1921. In consequence possibly of this inactivity the Wana Wazirs, assisted by certain Mahsud malcontents, became very much bolder, and roving gangs of hostile tribesmen began to give trouble along the lines of communication, and particularly on the section extending from Jandola to halfway between Dargai Oba and Rogha Kot.

On January 21st two officers of the Regiment were returning from Wana to Rogha Kot, where the whole of the 58th was now concentrated, escorted by six men mounted on mules. The little party had just passed a permanent picquet opposite the village of Hindi Kot, when shots were fired at very close range and the two men in the rear of the escort were seen to fall. The officers and the remaining four men dismounted and doubled back, but the enemy had wholly disappeared, and it seemed that the attackers must have crept down a deep nullah almost under the picquet, fired one volley and fled up the nullah to safety. Both the men who fell were killed.

The same evening just before dusk about forty of the enemy suddenly began sniping into the camp at Rogha Kot from Tora Tiza ridge, about 1,800 yards distant, making remarkably good shooting, while they had a large and varied target, the camp being full of transport animals as a convoy had only that day arrived. The ridge had not been picquetted, as it was thought too far off for enemy occupation, and there being no guns of any kind in camp, any retaliation was practically out of the question. The enemy must have expended some 500 rounds and the losses in camp amounted to one man killed and two wounded. There was also some loss among the animals, and Colonel Lind's charger was killed ; this had been all through the Great War, having been taken to France by Captain W. McM. Black, who was killed in the trenches on October 31st, 1914.

On February 1st, 1921, Brigadier-General A. A. J. Johnstone was gazetted Honorary Colonel of the Regiment.

Early in March it was made known that Wana would be occupied for certainly some months longer, and that a readjustment of troops would now take place. On the 14th the Regiment moved from Rogha Kot to Wana, which was then evacuated by the remainder of the troops which up to this had occupied it, these all proceeding to Sarwekai. This left the 58th Rifles in sole occupation of Wana, with a few sappers and miners to help in demolishing buildings no longer required for the reduced garrison, and in making the defences needed for the smaller garrison of some 550 rifles. Between Wana and Sarwekai, a post near Tanai was occupied by the 2nd Bn. 41st Dogras. The duties which now fell upon the Regiment were tolerably heavy ; permanent picquets to the number of eight, and each averaging a rifle strength of twelve, had to be occupied, while daily escorts were required for convoys passing over seven miles of road.

The situation was not a comfortable one, since the enemy, against whom no offensive action had been taken during the past two and a half months, was in a very aggressive mood. He had made up his mind that our troops were about to leave the country, and he was "all out" to give them as bad a time as he could. Several large bodies of hostile tribesmen were known to be in the neighbourhood, and the absence of punishment had made them bold.

On March 17th the up and down convoys met at the old Rogha Kot camp. The road protection troops from Wana and Tanai had established communication ; the down convoy from Wana had passed through, and the up convoy was about half a mile west of Rogha Kot when it was fired into at close range. By some misunderstanding an important hill had not been occupied by the Tanai troops, and the enemy, quick to notice the omission, had promptly seized the hill, was holding it in strength, and from it was pouring a heavy fire into the convoy. The leading company of the 58th managed to establish itself on a ridge some 300 yards from the enemy, and a permanent picquet of the Regiment, on the far bank of the stream and some 1,100 yards distant, gave useful support with its Lewis gun.

Having made the best dispositions possible under the circumstances, Lieutenant Jenkins very gallantly went in among the camels with his orderly, No. 3419 Sepoy Rasila, disentangled the leading camels, managed to get the sarwans to help, set the convoy on the move again, and kept it going until it was clear of the enemy's fire. In the meantime his signaller, No. 1029 Sepoy Kartar Singh, who had hitherto been unable to open communication with the Tanai troops, now very gallantly came out into the open to try to get a message through, but was killed while in the act of sending it.

Having got the convoy clear, Lieutenant Jenkins crossed the zone of fire and established touch with the Tanai troops, and by concerted action of the two bodies the hill was seized and the enemy ejected.

In this affair the casualties of the Regiment were 1 man killed and 2 wounded, while 2 camel drivers were killed and 3 wounded, and some 37 camels were killed and wounded.

Lieutenant Jenkins was awarded the Military Cross for his services. Sepoy Kartar Singh the Second Class of the Indian Order of Merit, the monetary value of the pension being granted to his widow for life; and Sepoy Rasila received the Indian Distinguished Service Medal.

From now onwards the tribesmen continued to be very aggressive; convoys were daily sniped; at night hundreds of yards of telephone wire were cut and removed, and on March 30th the up convoy to Wana was so very heavily sniped from the slopes of Michan Baba that two sepoys were wounded, while some fifty camels were killed and wounded.

A section of guns was now added to the garrison of Wana.

During this month the Depot of the Regiment was moved from Multan to Sialkote.

About this time certain steps had been taken in the direction of the re-organization of the Indian Army, and it was announced that Indian infantry regiments would for the future be grouped together in twenty-five "Indian Infantry Groups," each containing from four to five "Service" battalions and one "Training" battalion; and it was also stated that the 58th Rifles was to become the "Training" battalion of the group of which it was to form part. This would have meant that the Regiment would have become a mere depot battalion, thus altogether losing its individuality and entailing its complete disappearance as a fighting unit. Happily other counsels prevailed, and the Regiment was ultimately saved from the fate by which it was threatened, through the decision which was later come to to have a certain number of groups containing six instead of five battalions, while retaining certain of the second battalions raised during the Great War for employment as training battalions.

During April there were several encounters with the enemy. On the 5th he made an attempt to capture the down convoy and an action ensued; but the guard was not in sufficient strength to dislodge the tribesmen from the position they had taken up and the convoy had to retrace its steps, the escort holding the enemy off in a rearguard action, in which four sepoys were wounded; Subadar Kehr Singh, commanding a platoon on the exposed flank, behaved with conspicuous coolness and gallantry, for which he was later awarded the Indian Distinguished Service Medal.

On the following day there was an action of a more important character. A picquet of "C" Company—twenty-eight rifles and two Lewis guns under Havildars Jiwan Singh and Lal Singh—was sent to occupy a high hill known as Tora Tizha on the right bank of the stream, situated at and above the road point where the convoy escorts usually met. The hill was a spur of the main range and ran parallel to the river for nearly two miles. The only approach to the hill from the Wana sector was by a spur narrowing at the summit to a neck some 150 yards wide, and completely dominated by the top of the height. The summit consisted of a shelf of rock intersected with clefts and crevices, affording excellent cover from fire.

The picquet moved forward in four lines, covered by two guns of the 85th Mountain Battery, and on reaching the above-mentioned neck Havildar Jiwan Singh's platoon, which was leading, suddenly came under heavy and accurate rifle fire, whereby the whole of the accompanying Lewis gun section was wiped out, while at the same time some forty Wazirs, armed with knives, charged down upon the right flank. Supported by the platoon under Havildar Lal Singh, the attack was beaten off and heavy loss inflicted on the assailants, while another party that was coming down on the left flank was driven back by hand-grenades. The casualties sustained by the first volleys had reduced the strength of the 58th party to fourteen rifles and one Lewis gun only, but though faced by some 200 Wazirs strongly posted at a distance of no more than 200 yards, the picquet took up a position and held its ground for over an hour, when reinforcements came up. Another party of fifty Mahsuds who were advancing were dispersed by artillery fire.

Additional troops were hurried up from both sections, but though these were unable to drive the Mahsuds from the very strong position they occupied, the convoy was able to pass along, and the troops withdrew unmolested about 5 p.m., having suffered a loss of 6 men killed or died of wounds and 8 men wounded. Of the enemy, 8 killed and 4 wounded were actually counted, while two rifles were captured from him.

Havildar Jiwan Singh was awarded the Second Class of the Indian Order of Merit, while Havildar Lal Singh received the Indian Distinguished Service Medal.

Certain changes were made in the siting of some of the posts on the line and one or two new posts were established, making communications very much safer, and henceforth the passage of convoys was seldom interfered with. Further, a squadron of the 17th Cavalry was now ordered up to and stationed at Wana, making a very welcome and useful addition to the garrison.

During the third week in May information came in that some of the more urgently " wanted " of the local Wazirs had lately returned from Shahwal and Birmal to their homes for the purpose of husbanding their crops, and it was decided to carry out certain minor operations.

Accordingly, on the night of May 21st and 22nd the Regiment moved out to the western side of the Spin Warsak Ridge, and before dawn had occupied positions along some two miles of its length. At daybreak the squadron of the 17th Cavalry came out from Wana and swept through the villages between Wana and Spin Warsak, driving before them many armed Wazirs who all made for the ridge, which they found already in occupation by the 58th Rifles. Two Mahsuds were killed and 15 wounded, while the cavalry rounded up a number

H 2

of prisoners of whom some sixty—including several "wanted" men—were retained; two of the Regiment were wounded.

The Brigade Commander, Colonel Borrett, who was present during the greater part of the operations, congratulated the Regiment on the skilful manner in which the affair had been managed, expressing his entire satisfaction at the quiet maintained and the good march discipline of all the troops engaged.

When, on June 1st, the commander of the Waña force, Major-General T. Matheson, C.B., C.M.G., visited Wana to hold a jirga, the road protection troops were very heavily fired on from the slopes of Kotkum, while on their way down to meet the G.O.C.; but guns were quickly in action and the enemy dislodged. That evening when the jirga assembled the Regiment provided a Guard of Honour of seventy rifles for the force commander, who expressed his satisfaction at the smartness and turn-out of the Guard.

Early in June the Regiment marched from Wana to Dargai Oba, exchanging quarters with the 2nd Bn. 41st Dogras, and moved on October 7th up to Rogha Kot, where it relieved the 4th Bn. 3rd Gurkhas.

On November 1st Captain N. G. R. Coats, 25th Punjabis, reported his arrival on being posted as a permanent company commander; and on the 7th Major and Brevet Lieut.-Colonel J. D. M. Flood came out from leave in England and took over command of the Regiment from Major R. de W. Waller, D.S.O.

During the early part of this year great progress had been made in the disbanding of the regiments of Indian infantry raised during the war, and by the end of May some forty infantry and pioneer battalions had already been broken up, leaving some twenty-two others remaining to be disbanded as opportunity occurred. At the same time the re-organization of the Indian Army into groups of battalions was being carried out. A Special Indian Army Order dated November 24th, 1921, gives the permanent postings of commandants, seconds-in-command and company commanders to the majority of units of the post-war Indian infantry, and from this it may be seen that the composition of the 13th of these groups was as under:—

1st Bn. (55th Coke's Rifles), Frontier Force.

2nd Bn. (1st/5th Punjabi Rifles), Frontier Force.

3rd Bn. (57th Wilde's Rifles), Frontier Force.
4th Bn. (58th Vaughan's Rifles), Frontier Force.
5th Bn. (59th Royal Scinde Rifles), Frontier Force.
Training Battalion (2nd/56th Punjabi Rifles), Frontier Force.

Shortly after the arrival of the Regiment at Rogha Kot it was decided to withdraw all Regular troops from the Jandola—Wana line, replacing them by local levies, and on November 30th the withdrawal commenced, the 58th taking up a position across the valley midway between Wana and Rogha Kot to cover the retirement of the 4th Bn. 3rd Gurkhas from Wana. The enemy attempted to molest the latter corps, but was held by the dispositions made by the Regiment, and thereafter the withdrawal was carried out successively—to Dargai Oba on December 2nd, to Sarwekai on the 4th and to Haidari Kach on the 7th. Here the Regiment remained for ten days while stores and ammunition, etc., were being brought back to Jandola. On December 18th all troops having left Sarwekai, the force withdrew to Chagmalai, the Regiment providing the rearguard, and on arrival at Jandola about the 20th the Wana Force was broken up and the units composing it dispersed to their several garrisons.

The Regiment was now disposed as follows :—At Tank, 8 British officers, 7 Indian officers and 389 Indian other ranks, and at Kaur Bridge 4 British officers, 4 Indian officers and 207 non-commissioned officers and men.

The following was published by the G.O.C. on the breaking up of the Wana Force :—

"*On the dispersal of the Wana Column after more than a year's active service, Colonel Commandant O. C. Borrett, C.M.G., A.D.C., wishes to express to all ranks his pleasure in having commanded for nine months so fine a force.*

"*The excellent morale and offensive spirit of the troops have been no less marked than their ready acceptance of discomfort, disappointment, climatic extremes and sickness, and their cheerful endurance of hardships. It only remains to add that he has no more sincere hope than to command once more on still more active operations those troops which have so conspicuously demonstrated their soldierly qualities and fighting value.*"

The under-noted awards and mentions were made for services rendered :—

Mentioned in Despatches.—Lieut.-Colonel A. G. Lind, Majors R. de W. Waller (twice) and J. D. M. Flood, Captains R. G. Ekin, P. B. Ashton and P. P. Abernethy (twice), Subadar Mahammed Arbi, I.O.M., and No. 4903 Naik Abe Singh.

Second Class of the Order of British India, with the title of Bahadur.—Subadar Thakur Singh.

Indian Meritorious Service Medal.—Havildar-Major Ganga Singh, Naiks Sardar Khan and Bhagat Ram, Lance-Naik Habib Khan, Sepoys Suchta Singh, Santa Singh and Bhagat Singh.

On January 24th, 1922, a patrol composed of two Lewis gunners and two riflemen under Naik Sadda Khan was ambushed by some sixty Mahsuds when patrolling the road near Kaur Manzai in a Ford motor van. Both Lewis gunners were killed and both riflemen wounded, but the Naik got his wounded out of the van and covered their retirement until a reinforcement came up and drove the enemy off.

On February 11th the Regiment finally left the Waziristan border, and moved by rail and march route *via* Kalabagh, Mari Indus and Havelian to Abbottabad, where it arrived on the 14th, its departure being speeded by the following letter of good wishes from the G.O.C. Waziristan Force :—

" *I much regret that I have not an opportunity of saying good-bye to your Battalion before you leave the Wazir Force. You have been in the force for one year and eight months, most of which was spent with the Wana Column.*

" *The Battalion did line of communication duty between Sorarogha and Ladha from June to November,* 1920. *You advanced with the Wana Column in November,* 1920, *and you held Wana and outposts on the line of communication between December,* 1920, *and December,* 1921.

" *In December,* 1921, *you took part in the withdrawal from Wana to Jandola. Since then you have been doing garrison duty at Tank, Kaur and Dera Ismail Khan. You have been engaged in several successful actions, notably :—*

WANA KEEP, 1920

13th FRONTIER FORCE RIFLES, REUNION. ABBOTTABAD, 1927

" *At Wana Toi on April 5th*, 1921.

" *At Tora Tizha on April 6th*, 1921.

" *Rounding up of Shin Warsak on May 22nd*, 1921.

" *In all the operations and actions your Battalion has acquitted itself with credit and has added to its fine reputation. I congratulate your Battalion on its smartness, discipline and steadiness in action. I wish you all every luck in the future, when I am confident that you will add to the fine reputation you have won in Waziristan.*"

In 1922 the following Indian officers were granted Honorary King's Commissions in recognition of Distinguished Service :—

Subadar-Major Mir Alam Khan, Sirdar Bahadur, late 58th Rifles, to be Honorary Captain, with effect from July 1st, 1922.

Subadar-Major Gujar Singh, Bahadur, 58th Rifles, to be Honorary Lieutenant, with effect from December 8th, 1922.

In this year Brigadier-General A. A. J. Johnstone, the Honorary Colonel of the Regiment, presented a very handsome shield to be competed for annually by the companies of the Battalion. The shield was to remain in the Officers' Mess, the winning company receiving a monetary reward of Rs.200. The competition took the form of the gaining of marks in certain named events which included athletic sports, musketry and other competitions of a military character. Since its institution it has been won :—

In 1922-23 by " C " Company (Sikhs).

In 1923-24 by " C " Company (Sikhs).

In 1924-25 by " A " Company (Dogras).

During the year the following officers joined the Regiment :—

Major D. McL. Slater, from the 11th Rajputs, as company commander, and Lieutenant E. J. Denholm-Young, from the 28th Punjabis.

In furtherance of the Group System of Indian Army re-organization, the following was published on December 5th, 1922, under Indian Army Order No. 878 :—

" *Organization, Indian Army.*—Permanent numbers and titles for Indian Infantry and Pioneer regiments and battalions. Gazette of India Notification No. 1997, dated December 1st, 1922, on the above subject, is republished as an annexure to the Order.

"ORGANIZATION.

"INDIAN ARMY.

"His Majesty the King Emperor has been graciously pleased to approve of the following permanent numbers and titles for Indian Infantry and Pioneer regiments and battalions, consequent on re-organization and the introduction of the regimental system into the Indian Army.

"The new numbers and titles will have effect from the date of this notification.

* * * * *

"*Present Group.*	*Present Nos. and Titles of Battalions.*	*Future Nos. and Titles of Regts.*	*Future Nos. and Titles of Battalions.*
XIII.	1st Bn. 55th Coke's Rifles (F.F.)	13th Frontier Force Rifles	1st Bn. 13th Frontier Force Rifles (Coke's).
	1st Bn. 56th Punjabi Rifles (F.F.)		2nd Bn. 13th Frontier Force Rifles.
	57th Wilde's Rifles (F.F.)		4th Bn. 13th Frontier Force Rifles (Wilde's).
	58th Vaughan's Rifles (F.F.)		5th Bn. 13th Frontier Force Rifles (Vaughan's).
	59th Royal Scinde Rifles (F.F.)		6th Royal Bn. 13th Frontier Force Rifles (Scinde).
	2nd Bn. 56th Punjabi Rifles (F.F.)		10th Bn. 13th Frontier Force Rifles."

In the earlier grouping the 58th had been designated the 4th Battalion of the 13th Group, but under the present scheme the battalions of the Group were numbered from 1 to 2, 4 to 6 and 10, with the happy result that each regiment in becoming a battalion of the Group, reverted to the old regimental number under which it had originally been raised. The Training Battalion was numbered 10th in order to allow for the raising and numbering of five new battalions in the event of another Great War on as large a scale as the last.

The title of the Group—"Frontier Force Rifles"—led to the issue of an order for the general adoption by all battalions of a Rifle uniform and Rifle drill.

The composition of each battalion of the Group was fixed as under :—

One company of Sikhs.

One company of Dogras.

One company of Punjabi Mahammedans.

One company of Pathans, this last to be composed of two platoons of Khattaks, one platoon of Yusafzais and one of Afridis.

In order to bring the 5th Battalion—as the Regiment must now be called—up to establishment in the above-named classes, two platoons of Dogras were transferred from the 52nd Sikhs, Frontier Force, and two platoons of Khattaks from the 28th Punjabis.

Early in the year 1922 the 2nd Bn. 56th Rifles, now to become the 10th or Training Battalion of the 13th Frontier Force Rifles, was sent to Abbottabad, where it was to be permanently located. This battalion absorbed what was formerly the " Drill " of an active battalion, *viz.*, the instructional staff for recruits and the recruits themselves, all the recruits of the Group now being trained under the same system ; while in case of war any of the active battalions on field service will automatically be reinforced by men of the Group or Regiment, trained by its own officers— a very much more satisfactory arrangement than that which was followed in 1914-18, when regiments were often reinforced by men from units enlisting a totally different class of men.

On October 23rd, 1924, a War Memorial to all units of the old Punjab Frontier Force, which had been erected at Kohat, was unveiled by General Sir William Birdwood, Bart., G.C.B., G.C.M.G., K.C.S.I., C.I.E., D.S.O., who at the time was officiating as Commander-in-Chief in India. The Memorial had been raised by subscriptions from all units of the force, the Battalion subscribing Rs.2,200. Representative parties from all units—cavalry, artillery and infantry—were present under the command of Colonel P. L. Beddy, C.M.G., D.S.O., commanding 6th Indian Infantry (Kohat) Brigade. The Commander-in-Chief arrived on the ground at 10 a.m., accompanied by Major-General C. A. C. Godwin, C.M.G., D.S.O., the senior Punjab Frontier Force officer present.

Before unveiling the Memorial, the Commander-in-Chief addressed the troops in Urdu and English, and afterwards the buglers of the 3rd Bn. 12th Frontier Force Regiment sounded the "Last Post," which was followed by Chopin's "Funeral March" by the massed bands, and the "Flowers of the Forest" played by the pipers of the 3rd Bn. 12th Frontier Force Regiment. The buglers then sounded the "Réveillé" and the bands played "Land of Hope and Glory," while General Sir William Birdwood placed a wreath at the base of the Memorial, and the representative parties then marched past the Memorial. This is in the form of an obelisk about thirty feet in height, standing on a plinth, approached on the north over a small bridge and on the south by a flight of five steps.

The following is the text of the speech made by General Sir William Birdwood :—

"I am very glad to be able to be in Kohat to-day, and to have what I consider to be the great privilege of unveiling this Memorial which has been erected to the memory of those who belonged to regiments of the old Punjab Frontier Force, and who gave their lives during the recent Great War.

"I always feel that every soldier must be proud to be present on such an occasion, for we, who had the honour to be privileged to represent our Empire in the Great War, and who are fortunate enough to have returned safely, must, every one of us, realize that the eventual victory which was vouchsafed us was primarily due to those who did not return but who gave their lives—and, I believe, gave them willingly —in the cause for which we fought. We all of us realized that we were fighting in an entirely just and righteous cause. We only drew the sword with reluctance, and then only because honour and justice compelled us to do so, to uphold the liberty and freedom of our country and our people.

"I personally feel that there is no monument which I could unveil with greater pride than the one now before us, for it has been erected to the memory of regiments which perhaps more than any others in the Indian Army have made that Army, of which we are all so proud, famous throughout our great Empire, and even beyond its limits. The regiments concerned are all those belonging to the old Punjab Frontier Force, *viz.*, 21st, 22nd, 23rd and 25th Cavalry, the Corps of

Guides, the 21st, 22nd, 23rd and 24th Indian Mountain Batteries, 51st, 52nd, 53rd, 54th Sikhs, 55th, 56th, 57th, 58th and 59th Rifles and the 5th Gurkha Rifles. After enumerating those titles which have become so famous in the history of India, it must obviously be unnecessary, and indeed impossible, to go into details of their past histories, for they contain the history of the Indian Army since the year 1846. We know how entirely faithful all have proved themselves to the British Raj through times of terrible trouble, such as the Mutiny in 1857, and in all the wars in which our Empire has been engaged since those days, in Afghanistan, China and from one end of the North-West Frontier to the other. During the last great war every regiment of the Frontier Force added further to its glory and increased its already illustrious reputation. Again, I will not go into details, and I will only mention that various units took part in operations in all theatres of war—France, Mesopotamia, Palestine, Gallipoli, Egypt, Africa and the Frontier. During these operations they sustained the following casualties:—Killed: 171 officers, 122 sardars and 3,425 men. These figures speak for themselves, and no eloquence of mine or anyone else could do justice to what they tell us. We know that it was not strategy nor tactics nor leadership that really gained us the victory, but the spirit of sacrifice, and it is to that spirit of sacrifice which inspired these officers and men of the Frontier Force to pay the supreme price, that this monument is raised. There are few here who were not acquainted with at least some of them, and there are some who loved them very dearly, and one and all, relatives, comrades, friends, are assembled here with one object, to do honour to their memory, and display by our presence that we realize that it is they who have immortalized the part which the Frontier Force played in the greatest war of history. Let us not doubt for a moment that the manner of their death was worthy of the greatness of their sacrifice. They were weak mortals like ourselves, with all the frailties that belong to us, but we believe—and some of us know—that when All-Merciful God sends out to men the summons to meet death, He also sends out a strengthening courage to enable them to meet it, as brave soldiers always will do. In honouring the dead let us, who have returned sound in mind and limb, not forget our less fortunate comrades who have returned to their homes maimed and possibly broken down in health, and perhaps with inadequate means or pensions, and let us determine to do anything that may be in our power to help them and look after their interests.

"I now unveil this Memorial to the glory of God, and in memory of those brave men who gave their lives for their country."

On the same day General Birdwood unveiled in St. Augustine's Church, Kohat, Memorial Tablets bearing the names of all British officers of the Punjab Frontier Force who had given their lives in the Great War. The Regiment's tablet bears the following names :—

Lieut.-Colonel W. E. Venour, Lieut.-Colonel C. E. Davidson-Houston, D.S.O., Captain H. L. C. Baldwin, Captain C. H. Elliot, Captain G. S. Bull, M.C., Captain W. McM. Black, Captain R. B. Kitson, Captain F. E. Hodgson, Captain A. Flagg, Captain K. B. Mackenzie, Captain D. R. Montford, Lieutenant L. Gaisford, Lieutenant J. H. Milligan, Lieutenant J. O. Nicolls, Lieutenant B. Douglas, Lieutenant R. A. Reilly, Lieutenant Macmillan, Lieutenant J. Mackay and 2nd-Lieutenant F. B. Deane-Spread.

On this occasion General Sir William Birdwood delivered the following dedicatory address :—

"I deem it a great honour to be able to unveil this Memorial Tablet. More especially do I feel this to be the case in this little church in which I was privileged to be a humble worshipper for many years, and every stone of which I feel I love. In those days the mural tablets around us were very much fewer, for, alas ! the recent wars have added so greatly to their numbers. Nor were there then any of these regimental Colours, which we now see on the wall of the church—Colours which mean so very much to us, embodying as they do all our great traditions, and reminding us of all those many brave men who have given their lives in defending them. When I see them my mind instinctively goes back to old school days, and I expect there are many here present who, like me, remember that beautiful anthem, which is, I think, sung in many of our schools at home—the anthem from Ecclesiasticus beginning 'Let us now praise famous men, there be of them that have left a name behind them that their deeds should be remembered among men.' Then later on the anthem goes 'But some there be who have no memorial.' With those words I expect the minds of many of us will at once go back to comrades whom we have known, who have perhaps been alongside of us one moment, to be gone the next, perhaps blown to pieces; or perhaps to some, who have been torpedoed, or who for any other reason we have been unable to honour with a definite resting place. So that we should not be unduly distressed at this, the anthem later goes on with the words 'Their name liveth for evermore,' and indeed we do know they live for evermore in the hearts of their people among the honoured ones of our nation. They have joined the empire of the silent dead, who though silent, speak to the whole world.

"I think there are probably many here present who feel with me that they who have gone before us, know that we are assembled here to-day, and that their sacrifice has not been in vain. They know, as we soldiers know, that this simple military service, the familiar bugle calls we recently heard, have a special significance to us. The 'Last Post' which was sounded was a tribute to our honoured dead, and the 'Réveillé' which followed was the proclamation of our sure and certain hope of their resurrection to eternal life.

"I am sure we can feel that there are many of those whose names are on the Memorial I am about to unveil, of whom we can think what I always regard as such beautiful words from Thackeray, 'And then his spirit, which was as that of a little child, returned to him who gave it.'

"I now unveil this Memorial to the glory of God, and to the memory of our comrades of the Frontier Force, who have given their lives for their country."

At the ceremony there was a large gathering of old Indian officers, non-commissioned officers and men from all units of the Force, and it was a very pleasant reunion of past and present members. Amongst the pensioners of the Battalion present was Subadar Zard Ali Khan, Bahadur (Yusafzai), who at the time was unfortunately too ill to be presented to General Sir William Birdwood. Although he was in ill health the Subadar insisted on coming from his village to be present; he met many old friends and received much sympathy from all on account of his state of health. He was a fine type of the old Indian officer, devoted to the Regiment which had been his home for just thirty-three years. He died very shortly after arrival back at his village.

The Battalion remained in Abbottabad until the autumn of 1924, being joined during this year by 2nd-Lieutenant E. D. Tims, 2nd Bn. The Devonshire Regiment, on being posted to the Indian Army. While stationed at Abbottabad the Battalion furnished a detachment of one complete company at Attock for the protection of the Fort and Bridge, from September, 1922, to September, 1923, and again from July to October, 1924.

In the programme of reliefs for 1924-25 the Battalion was down as to be sent to Kohat and outposts, and the G.O.C. Kohat District decided that the Battalion should spend its first two years in this district on outpost duty, and it was accordingly ordered to Thal, arriving there by train on October 29th and relieving the 2nd Bn. 9th Jat Infantry.

The following was published in Rawal Pindi District Orders of October 25th, 1924 :—

" *On the departure of the 5th Bn. 13th Frontier Force Rifles (58th) for the Kohat District, the District Commander wishes to place on record his appreciation of the good work done by the Battalion since its arrival in the District from Waziristan in February,* 1922.

" *The bearing and spirit of all ranks has been admirable and typical of the best traditions of the Frontier Force.*

" *The District Commander is confident that this high reputation will be maintained in whatever station the Battalion may serve, and he wishes Lieut.-Colonel Lind and all ranks under his command the best of good luck.*"

On May 20th, 1925, the Headquarters and two companies—later relieved by the two others—marched to Parachinar, returning to Thal on October 28th ; the change to the cool climate of Parachinar was greatly appreciated after the heat and cramped surroundings of Thal.

During this year Captain J. B. Smalley was posted to the Battalion on the disbandment of the 2nd Bn. 55th Coke's Rifles, while the following promotions were announced in the India Gazette of 1925 :—

To the First Class of the Order of British India with the Title of Sirdar Bahadur.—Subadar-Major and Honorary Captain Gujar Singh, Bahadur, 5th Bn. 13th Frontier Force Rifles.

To the Second Class of the Order of British India with the Title of Bahadur.—Subadar Mahammed Arbi, Indian Order of Merit, 5th Bn. 13th Frontier Force Rifles.

In this year also a further and unusual honour was conferred upon two members of the Battalion, the Macgregor Memorial Medals being awarded to Captain C. R. Spear and No. 4542 Naik Jabbar Khan (Bangash Khattak) for highly creditable reconnaissance work carried out at no small personal risk. In the case of Captain Spear the work was conducted in China and Mongolia, and in the case of the non-commissioned officer in Afghanistan.

On February 1st, 1926, Lieut.-Colonel A. G. Lind, D.S.O., vacated the command of the Battalion and was succeeded by Major R. de W. Waller, D.S.O.

Twenty squares of land in the Nili Bar Canal Colony were, on March 19th, given to the Regiment, and were apportioned among four Indian officers—Subadars Kehr Singh, Sohnu and Khan Bahadur, and Jemadar Sirdar Khan—and fifteen non-commissioned officers and men.

During the month of March the Headquarters and two companies of the Battalion were employed for some ten days at Arawali on protection duty in connection with the Royal Air Force concentration at that place.

On October 30th, 1926, the stay of the Battalion at Thal and Parachinar came to an end, and on that day, having been relieved by the 4th Bn. 13th Frontier Force Rifles, it proceeded by train to Kohat where on arrival it was quartered in the Lockhart Lines.

APPENDICES

APPENDIX A.

THE GREAT WAR.

BRITISH OFFICERS KILLED.

Name	Date
Lieut.-Colonel W. E. Venour	Oct. 31st, 1914
Capt. W. McM. Black	„ 31st, 1914
Lieut. J. McA. Craig, 57th Rifles, Frontier Force (attd.)	„ 31st, 1914
Capt. H. L. C. Baldwin	Nov. 23rd, 1914
Lieut. L. Gaisford	„ 23rd, 1914
Lieut. R. A. Reilly, 31st Punjabis (attd.)	„ 23rd, 1914
Capt. M. A. R. Bell, 54th Sikhs, Frontier Force (attd.) ...	Dec. 20th, 1914
Capt. C. H. Elliot	April 27th, 1915
Lieut. S. A. MacMillan, I.A.R.O. (attd.), died of wounds	May 9th, 1915
Capt. F. F. Hodgson, 84th Punjabis (attd.)	„ 17th, 1915
Lieut.-Colonel C. E. D. Davidson-Houston, D.S.O. ...	Sept. 25th, 1915
Capt. J. H. Milligan	„ 25th, 1915
Lieut. T. O. Nicolls	„ 25th, 1915
Capt. A. Flagg, I.A.R.O. (attd.)	„ 25th, 1915
Capt. K. B. Mackenzie, 123rd Rifles (attd.)	„ 25th, 1915
2/Lieut. F. B. Deane-Spread, I.A.R.O. (attd.)	„ 25th, 1915
Capt. R. B. Kitson	Nov. 11th, 1917
Lieut. B. Douglas, 101st Grenadiers (attd.)	„ 13th, 1917
Capt. D. R. Montford, 98th Infantry (attd.), missing, believed died of wounds	Mar. 30th, 1918
Lieut. J. Mackay, I.A.R.O. (attd.)	„ 30th, 1918

BRITISH OFFICERS WOUNDED.

Name	Date
Capt. A. G. Lind	Nov. 23rd, 1914
Capt. E. S. C. Willis, D.S.O.	„ 23rd, 1914
Capt. C. H. Elliot	Dec. 10th, 1914
Capt. C. G. V. M. Wardell, 21st Punjabis (attd.)	Mar. 11th, 1915
Capt. E. Grose, 16th Rajputs (attd.)	„ 11th, 1915
Capt. A. A. Smith	„ 12th, 1915
Capt. J. Y. Tancred, 19th Punjabis (attd.)	April 25th, 1915
Capt. G. S. Bull	May 9th, 1915
Major A. G. Thomson	„ 9th, 1915
Lieut. J. H. Milligan	July 5th, 1915
Capt. C. B. Harcourt, 28th Punjabis (attd.) wounded and taken prisoner	Sept. 25th, 1915
Capt. C. G. V. M. Wardell, 21st Punjabis (attd.)	„ 25th, 1915
Major R. de W. Waller	Nov. 19th, 1917
Lieut. S. T. Gray, I.A.R.O. (attd.)	April 10th, 1918
2/Lieut. A. H. C. Allen, 2nd Bn. 4th Devon Regt. (attd.) ...	Sept. 19th, 1918

INDIAN OFFICERS KILLED.

Name	Date
Subadar Wazir Singh	Nov. 25th, 1914
Jemadar Mardan Ali	Dec. 20th, 1914
Subadar Phuman Singh, I.D.S.M., died of wounds ...	Feb. 13th, 1915
Subadar Bostan Khan, 82nd Punjabis (attd.)	May 9th, 1915
Jemadar Lal Khan, 82nd Punjabis (attd.)	„ 9th, 1915
Jemadar Rakmat	„ 17th, 1915
Subadar Sohel Singh, I.O.M.	Sept. 25th, 1915
Jemadar Yar Dil	„ 25th, 1915
Jemadar Din Mahammed, 123rd Rifles (attd.)	„ 25th, 1915
Jemadar Fazl Dad, I.D.S.M.	Nov. 1st, 1917
Subadar Lal Khan, I.O.M.	Mar. 30th, 1918

INDIAN OFFICERS WOUNDED.

Name	Date
Subadar Khan Bahadur	Oct. 31st, 1914
Subadar Abdul Ali	„ 31st, 1914
Jemadar Sohel Singh	„ 31st, 1914
Subadar Saiyid Gul	Nov. 15th, 1914
Subadar Abdul Ali Bahadur (second time)	„ 22nd, 1914
Subadar Gujar Singh	„ 23rd, 1914
Subadar Phuman Singh, I.D.S.M.	Feb. 6th, 1915
Subadar Indar Singh, M.C., I.D.S.M.	Mar. 6th, 1915
Subadar Karam Singh, I.O.M.	„ 9th, 1915
Jemadar Hira Singh	May 9th, 1915
Jemadar Kehr Singh	„ 9th, 1915
Jemadar Abdul Rahman	„ 9th, 1915
Jemadar Hawindah, M.C., I.D.S.M.	„ 9th, 1915
Subadar Hamid Khan, I.D.S.M.	„ 17th, 1915
Jemadar Mir Zaman, 66th Punjabis (attd.)	„ 17th, 1915
Jemadar Mahammed Arbi, I.O.M.	„ 18th, 1915
Jemadar Yar Dil	„ 18th, 1915
Jemadar Hukmat	June 4th, 1915
Jemadar Hamesh Gul	„ 4th, 1915
Jemadar Yar Dil (second time)	July 11th, 1915
Subadar Raj Talab Bahadur, I.D.S.M.	Aug. 6th, 1915
Subadar Lal Singh	Sept. 16th, 1915
Subadar Karam Dad, 123rd Outram's Rifles (attd.) ...	„ 25th, 1915
Jemadar Golodu, 54th Sikhs, Frontier Force (attd.) ...	Oct. 9th, 1915
Subadar Shah Sowar, 101st Grenadiers (attd.)	Nov. 13th, 1917
Jemadar Hussein Bux, 101st Grenadiers (attd.)	„ 13th, 1917
Jemadar Ahmad Din, 101st Grenadiers (attd.)	„ 13th, 1917
Subadar Karam Singh, I.O.M. (second time)	„ 14th, 1917
Jemadar Mirza Khan	Mar. 30th, 1918
Subadar Mahammed Arbi, I.O.M. (second time) ...	Sept. 19th, 1918

INDIAN OTHER RANKS.

Killed	288	Approximately 70 per cent. of these were exclusively 58th Rifles; remaining 30 per cent. men of other units attached.
Died of wounds	61	
Died of disease	46	Approximately 62 per cent. of these were exclusively 58th Rifles; remaining 38 per cent. men of other units attached.
Wounded ...	1,163	

TOTAL CASUALTIES.

	British Officers.	*Indian Officers.*	*Other Ranks.*
Killed	18	10	288
Died of wounds	2	1	61
Died of disease...	1	0	46
Wounded, missing and prisoners	15	30	1,163
Total Casualties	36	41	1,558

APPENDIX B.

HONOURS AND AWARDS GAINED DURING THE WAR, 1914-18, BY THE 58TH RIFLES.

Distinguished Service Order.

Lieut.-Colonel C. E. D. Davidson-Houston ...	France, 1914.
Major A. G. Thomson	France, 1915.
Capt. S. B. Pope	France, 1915.
Major A. G. Lind	Palestine, 1917.
Major R. de W. Waller...	Palestine, 1918.

Military Cross.

Capt. G. S. Bull	France, 1914.
Jemadar Indar Singh, I.D.S.M.	France, 1914.
Jemadar Hawindah	France, 1915.
Capt. S. Gordon, I.M.S.	France, 1915.
Capt. G. R. Dowland	Palestine, 1917.
Lieut. G. G. Hills	Palestine, 1918.

Indian Order of Merit, First Class.

Subadar Sohel Singh	France, 1915.
Subadar Mahammed Arbi Khan	Palestine, 1917.

Indian Order of Merit, Second Class.

Jemadar Sohel Singh	France, 1914.
No. 1811 Havildar Karam Singh	France, 1914.
Jemadar Harchand Singh	France, 1914.
No. 1848 Havildar Roshan Khan	France, 1914.
No. 3572 Havildar Saidak	France, 1914.
No. 3032 Havildar Lal Badshah	France, 1914.
No. 2823 Lance-Naik Sher Khan	France, 1914.
No. 2742 Sepoy Ishar Singh	France, 1914.
Jemadar Mahammed Arbi Khan	France, 1915.
No. 1925 Havildar Santa Singh	France, 1915.
No. 2830 Havildar Kashmir Singh	France, 1915.
No. 3131 Lance-Naik Phangan Singh ...	France, 1915.

Order of British India, Second Class.

Subadar Abdul Ali	France, 1914.
Subadar Rai Talab Khan	France, 1915.
Subadar-Major Tikka Khan	Palestine, 1917-18.
Subadar Gujar Singh	IndianFrontier,1917-18.

Indian Distinguished Service Medal.

Jemadar Hamid Khan ... ... France, 1914.
Jemadar Indar Singh, M.C. ... ... France, 1914.
No. 3404 Naik Baid Ullah ... ... France, 1914.
No. 2164 Havildar Sundar Singh ... ... France, 1914.
No. 2152 Havildar Lashkari ... ... France, 1914.
Subadar Rai Talab Khan ... ... France, 1914.
No. 2763 Havildar Ajun Khan ... ... France, 1914.
No. 3136 Havildar Sarfaraz ... ... France, 1914.
No. 2758 Naik Dewa Singh ... ... France, 1914.
No. 2634 Naik Zarghun Shah ... ... France, 1914.
No. 3133 Sepoy Maluk Singh ... ... France, 1914.
No. 3374 Sepoy Dewa Singh (bar in 1917) ... France, 1914.
No. 3080 Naik Zar Baz ... ... France, 1914.
Jemadar Hawindah ... ... France, 1914.
No. 3567 Lance-Naik Saiyid Asghar ... ... France, 1914.
Subadar Phunam Singh ... ... France, 1915.
No. 2198 Havildar Fazl Dad ... ... France, 1915.
No. 3066 Naik Sirdar Khan ... ... France, 1915.
No. 2934 Sepoy Mahammed Amin ... ... France, 1915.
No. 3323 Havildar Fazl Dad. ... ... Palestine, 1917.
No. 3835 Lance-Naik Rahim Ali ... ... Palestine, 1917.
No. 3374 Naik Dewa Singh (bar) ... ... Palestine, 1917.
No. 2927 Lance-Naik Bhag Singh ... ... Palestine, 1917.
No. 2841 Naik Wadhawa ... ... Palestine, 1918.
No. 3291 Sepoy Kapura ... ... Palestine, 1918.
No. 4341 Sepoy Jaimal Singh ... ... Palestine, 1918.
No. 4141 Sepoy Damodar ... ... Palestine, 1918.
No. 3704 Lance-Naik Diwan Singh ... ... Palestine, 1918.
No. 4778 Sepoy Bhola Singh ... ... Palestine, 1918.
No. 2938 Lance-Naik Pritam Singh ... ... Palestine, 1918.
No. 651 Sepoy Fairu ... ... Palestine, 1918.
No. 4263 Sepoy Bara Singh ... ... Palestine, 1918.
No. 4387 Sepoy Amar Singh ... ... Palestine, 1918.
No. 4707 Sepoy Hakim Singh ... ... Palestine, 1918.

FOREIGN DECORATIONS.

Russian.

Order of St. Stanislaus, Third Class.
Lieut.-Colonel E. R. B. Murray.

Cross of St. George, Fourth Class.
No. 3080 Naik Zar Baz.

Serbian.

Order of the White Eagle, Fifth Class.
Subadar Tikka Khan.

Silver Star.
No. 3722 Naik Redi Gul.

Gold Medal.
No. 3457 Naik Safirullah.

French.

Croix de Guerre.
Major A. G. Lind.

HONOURS AND AWARDS GAINED BY MEN OF OTHER CORPS SERVING WITH THE REGIMENT.

Military Cross.

2nd-Lieut. A. H. C. Allen, 2nd Bn. 4th Devonshire Regiment ... ... Palestine, 1918.

Indian Order of Merit, Second Class.

Subadar Lal Khan, 55th Rifles, Frontier Force Palestine, 1917.

Indian Distinguished Service Medal.

Subadar Ahmad Din, 1/101st Grenadiers ... Palestine, 1917.
No. 1873 Naik Mahammed Yasuf, 1/101st Grenadiers ... ... Palestine, 1917.
No. 1893 Sepoy Mahammed Khan, 1/101st Grenadiers ... ... Palestine, 1917.
No. 1177 Lance-Naik Gaur Ali, 1/101st Grenadiers ... ... Palestinę, 1917.
No. 1226 Sepoy Umar Khan, 1/101st Grenadiers Palestine, 1917.
No. 1968 Sepoy Dilbar Shah, 1/101st Grenadiers Palestine, 1917.
No. 4000 Sepoy Mahammed Khan, 2/101st Grenadiers ... ... Palestine, 1917.

SPECIAL REWARDS FOR SERVICE IN THE GREAT WAR.

Jagirs of Land.
Subadar Mahammed Arbi Khan.
Subadar-Major and Honorary Captain Mir Alam Khan, Sirdar Bahadur.

Special Assignment of Land Revenue.
Subadar Indar Singh, M.C., I.D.S.M.

Grants of Land.
19 assigned to Indian officers, each receiving two squares ; 66 to Indian other ranks.

Jangi Inams.
Two to Indian officers and 82 to Indian other ranks.

APPENDIX C.

LIST OF UNITS FROM WHICH REINFORCEMENTS WERE RECEIVED.

Date.	Unit.	B.O.	I.O.	O.R.
December, 1914	91st Punjabis*	1	2	204
12/2/1915 ...	82nd Punjabis	1	3	97
1/4/1915 ...	82nd Punjabis	—	1	31
1/4/1915 ...	54th Sikhs, Frontier Force	—	1	62
12/5/1915 ...	82nd Punjabis	—	—	49
12/5/1915 ...	66th Punjabis	—	—	11
18/6/1915 ...	76th Punjabis	—	—	26
26/8/1915 ...	123rd Outram's Rifles	2	4	162
5/3/1916 ...	55th Rifles, Frontier Force	—	1	138
9/2/1917 ...	55th Rifles, Frontier Force	1	6	218
24/10/1917 ...	101st Grenadiers	1	4	208
18/12/1917 ...	101st Grenadiers	1	2	74
21/3/1918 ...	98th Infantry...	2	3	205
18/10/1918 ...	57th Rifles, Frontier Force	1	0	74
9/12/1918 ...	57th Rifles, Frontier Force	—	2	110
	Total Reinforcements	10	29	1,669

The Regiment was thus reinforced by representatives of *ten* different units !

* This draft was composed of Dogras and was re-transferred after a few days to the 39th Garhwal Rifles.

APPENDIX D.

THE WORK OF THE DEPOT.

In addition to the reinforcements mentioned in the foregoing Appendix, sent to the Regiment from other corps, 1,661 Indian officers, non-commissioned officers and men were dispatched to the Regiment in the field from the Depot in India. The majority of these were enlisted and trained at the Depot, the remainder being either Reservists or trained men who, from one cause or another, had been left behind in India in September, 1914.

Between August, 1914, and November, 1918, the following numbers and classes of recruits were enlisted at the Depot :—

Sikhs	715
Punjabi Mahammedans	1,493
Dogras	250
Yusafzais	377
Afridis	90
Total	2,925

Besides the above, 426 Multanis were enlisted and trained at the Depot, these being later transferred to the 2nd Bn. 56th Rifles, Frontier Force, on the formation of that unit at Multan in July, 1917.

APPENDIX E.

ROLL OF OFFICERS OF THE 5TH PUNJAB INFANTRY, 58TH FRONTIER FORCE RIFLES AND 5TH BATTALION 13TH FRONTIER FORCE RIFLES, 1849-1926.

ABERNETHY, P. P. 2nd/Lieutenant, Unattached List, 13/1/17. Appointed to Indian Army, 7/2/17. Posted to 58th, 13/6/17 ; Lieutenant, 30/1/18 ; Captain, 30/1/21. Appointed Instructor, S.A. School, 18/1/25.

War of 1914-18 : Egyptian Expeditionary Force, 17/10/17 to 31/10/18 ; Waziristan, 1920-21, despatches twice.

ANDERSON, S. Surgeon-Captain, I.M.S., 28/7/00. Posted to 5th Punjab Infantry, 2/3/01 ; to Civil Employ in 1902.

ARNOLD, A. F. 2nd/Lieutenant, Unattached List, 29/1/20. Appointed to Indian Army, 5/2/20 ; Lieutenant, 21/1/21.

ASHTON, E. M. 2nd/Lieutenant, Royal Air Force, 15/5/15 ; Lieutenant, 16/4/16. Posted to 58th, 2/4/19 ; Captain, 15/6/19.

War of 1914-18 : Gallipoli, 10/8/15 to 17/8/15 (wounded) ; Egyptian Expeditionary Force, 10/5/16 to 21/3/18, despatches.

ASHTON, P. W. B. 2nd/Lieutenant, The Suffolk Regiment, 29/7/15 ; Lieutenant, 29/7/16. Posted to 58th, 5/11/17. Appointed to Indian Army 31/10/18 ; Captain, 29/7/19.

BABTIE, J. W. A. 2nd/Lieutenant, Army, 11/5/16 ; Lieutenant, 14/5/17. Appointed to Indian Army, 30/11/17. Posted to 58th, 5/12/17 ; Captain, 14/5/20.

War of 1914-18 ; Afghanistan, 1919 ; Waziristan, 1920-21.

BALDWIN, H. L. C. V. 2nd/Lieutenant, Unattached List, 20/7/98. Appointed Madras S. C., 15/10/99 ; Lieutenant, 20/10/00. Appointed 5th Punjab Infantry, 16/11/01 ; Captain, 20/7/07.

N.W. Frontier, 1901-02 ; N.W. Frontier, 1902 ; War of 1914-18 ; killed in action, 23/11/14.

BECKETT, S. Appointed Ensign, Indian Army, 13/6/57. Lieutenant, 25th Bengal N.I., 18/5/58. Appointed Adjutant 5th P.I., 18/4/63. Appointed 2nd Sikh Infantry, 22/2/64 ; Captain, 13/6/69 ; Major, 13/6/77 ; Lieut.-Colonel, 13/6/83 ; awarded C.B., 25/8/85 ; Colonel, 13/6/87 ; retired, 1/11/89.

Indian Mutiny, Oudh Campaign, 1858-59 (wounded), despatches ; N.W. Frontier, 1863, despatches twice ; Sudan, 1885, despatches, C.B.

BLACK, W. McM. 2nd-Lieutenant, Royal Scots Fusiliers, 7/5/02. Appointed Bengal S. C., 3/11/03 ; Lieutenant, 7/8/04. Posted to 58th, 30/6/06 ; Captain, 7/5/11.

War of 1914-18 ; killed in action, 31/10/14.

BROWNE, G. B. 2nd-Lieutenant, Unattached List, 15/9/97. Appointed Bengal S.C., 25/12/98 ; Lieutenant, 15/12/99 ; Captain, 15/9/06.

N.W. Frontier, 1901-02 ; N.W. Frontier, 1902 ; murdered at Tank, 12/4/14.

BULL, G. S. 2nd-Lieutenant, Royal Garrison Artillery, 25/6/99 ; Lieutenant, 16/4/01. Punjab S.C., 21/4/04. Posted to 58th, 21/4/04 ; Captain, 25/6/08.

War of 1914-18 (wounded) ; died at Suez, 25/3/16.

COATS, N. G. R. 2nd-Lieutenant, Unattached List, 9/9/08. Appointed to Indian Army, 7/11/09 ; Lieutenant, 9/12/10 ; Captain, 1/9/15. Posted to 5th Bn. 13th Frontier Force Rifles in 1922 ; Major, 9/9/24.

COLLINSON, W. J. Lieutenant, I.M.S., 1/9/02 ; Captain, 1/9/05. Posted to 5th P.I., 9/10/07 ; Major, 1/3/14 ; Lieut.-Colonel, 1/3/22.

War of 1914-18 : Egyptian Expeditionary Force, 17/11/14-18/3/16.

CONOLLY, A. Lieutenant, Royal Artillery, 8/6/60. Appointed Quartermaster, 5th P.I., 4/8/71 ; Captain, 1/7/75. Posted to Erinpura Irregular Infantry, 9/9/75 ; Major, 8/6/80 ; Lieut.-Colonel, 2/3/81 ; Colonel, 2/3/85 ; retired, 15/6/88.

N.W. Frontier, Ambela, 1863 ; Afghan War, 1878-80, despatches, Brevet Lieut.-Colonel.

COOPER, H. A. 2nd-Lieutenant, The Manchester Regiment, 29/8/85 ; Lieutenant same date. Appointed to Indian S.C. and posted to 5th P.I., 23/12/87. Posted to 1st Sikhs, 22/10/88 ; Captain, 29/8/96 ; Major, 29/8/03 ; died at Fyzabad, 5/1/05.

Hazara Expedition, 1888 ; Waziristan, 1894-95 ; Dongola Expedition, 1896, Bt. Major ; N.W. Frontier, 1897-98, despatches.

COOPER, L. E. 2nd-Lieutenant, 75th Foot, 13/8/79 ; 2nd-Lieutenant, 40th Foot, 27/9/79 ; Lieutenant, 1/7/81. Appointed to Indian Army, 24/9/82. Posted to 5th P.I., 11/1/84 ; Captain, 13/8/90. Posted to 2nd P.I., 4/3/96 ; Major, 13/8/99 ; Lieut.-Colonel, 2/4/01 ; died at Reading, 9/2/05.

N.W. Frontier, 1897-98, despatches.

COSTELLO, C. P. Assistant Surgeon, I.M.S., 10/2/59. Posted to 5th P.I., 24/8/60. Posted to 5th P.C., 25/8/65.

COURTNEY, S. C. Assistant Surgeon, I.M.S., 27/1/58. Posted to 5th P.I., 12/4/61. Posted to 1st P.C., 19/4/62.

CREAGH, R. C. O. Lieutenant, Royal Marine Light Infantry, 1/8/83. Appointed to Madras S.C., 1/8/83. Posted to 5th P.I., 12/11/88 ; Captain, 1/8/94 ; Major, 1/9/01 ; died at Netley, 27/1/04.

Burma War, 1887-88 ; Manipur Expedition, 1891 ; Chitral, 1895 ; N.W. Frontier, 1897-98 ; South African War, 1899-1900.

CREWE, R. Ensign, Indian Army, 13/12/33 ; 45th Madras N.I., 13/11/34 ; Lieutenant, 12/2/36 ; Captain, 20/12/43. D.A.A.G., Mysore Division, 10/10/48. Appointed Commandant 5th P.I., 1/4/51 ; Major, 20/6/54 ; Lieut.-Colonel, 6/6/56 ; Mil. Sec. to Governor, Madras, 1/4/59 ; Colonel, 28/2/61 ; Retired, 17/5/61.

CUMMING, A. E. 2nd-Lieutenant, Unattached List, 29/6/16. Appointed to Indian Army and posted to 58th, 2/7/16 ; Lieutenant, 28/12/16 ; Captain, 28/12/19.

War of 1914-18 : Mesopotamia, 17/3/17-31/12/17 ; Egyptian Expeditionary Force, 1/1/18-31/10/18, Military Cross.

CURTIS, O. O. 2nd-Lieutenant, Unattached List, 9/9/08. Appointed to Indian Army, 8/8/09 ; Lieutenant, 9/12/10 ; Captain, 1/9/15 ; G.S.O.3, 18/12/23-31/12/23 ; G.S.O.2, 1/1/24-7/11/24 ; Major, 9/9/24.

War of 1914-18, despatches ; Waziristan, 1924.

DAVIDSON-HOUSTON, C. E. D. 2nd-Lieutenant, Unattached List, 28/6/93. Appointed to Bengal S.C., 14/10/94 ; Lieutenant, 28/9/95. Posted to 5th P.I., 4/6/97 ; Adjutant, 1/6/01 ; Captain, 28/6/02 ; Major, 28/6/11 ; Commandant, 5th, 21/10/14 ; killed in action, 25/9/15.

N.W. Frontier, 1897-98 ; Waziristan, 1901-02 ; N.W. Frontier, 1902 (wounded) ; War of 1914-18, D.S.O.

DENHOLM-YOUNG, E. J. 2nd-Lieutenant, Unattached List, 16/12/18. Appointed to Indian Army, 12/1/19 ; Lieutenant, 16/1/19 ; Captain, 16/12/24.

DOUGAN, H. A. Lieutenant, I.M.S., 1/9/04. Posted to 58th, 15/10/06 ; Captain, 1/9/07. Posted to 109th Infantry, 15/10/08.

DOWLAND, G. R. 2nd-Lieutenant, Unattached List, 14/1/14. Appointed to Indian Army, 7/3/14. Posted to 58th, 15/10/14 ; Lieutenant, 1/9/15 ; Captain, 14/1/18.

War of 1914-18 ; Somaliland, 16/7/16-16/7/17. Egyptian Expeditionary Force, 17/7/18-31/10/18, Military Cross.

DUER, C. Surgeon-Captain, I.M.S., 28/7/91. Posted to 5th P.I., 11/11/95. Appointed Civil Surgeon, Burma, 25/9/00.

EALES, C. M. 2nd-Lieutenant, Royal Scots Fusiliers, 22/1/81. Madras S.C., 16/10/82. Posted to 5th P.I., 9/5/86. Posted to 2nd P.I., 22/8/87 ; Captain, 22/1/92 ; Major, 21/1/01 ; Lieut.-Colonel, 22/1/07 ; retired, same date.

N.W. Frontier, 1891 ; N.W. Frontier, 1894-95 ; N.W. Frontier, 1897-98, despatches.

ERSKINE, A. Ensign, 108th Foot, 20/12/58 ; Lieutenant, 2/11/63. Posted to 5th P.I., 30/12/67. Not traced after 1870.

EVANS, T. L. 2nd-Lieutenant, Unattached List, 21/12/17. Appointed to Indian Army, 20/3/18 ; Lieutenant, 21/12/18. Posted to 58th, 3/6/19 ; Captain, 21/12/22.

Waziristan, 1920-21.

FINLEY, R. F. 2nd-Lieutenant, Royal Artillery, 22/10/97; Lieutenant, 22/10/00. Posted to 15th Madras Infantry, 7/11/00; to 5th P.I., 28/4/01; Captain, 22/10/06; Major, 1/9/15; Bt. Lieut.-Colonel, 1/1/20; Lieut.-Colonel, 52nd Sikhs, 20/2/21; Colonel, 1/1/24; retired, 21/8/27. G.S.O.3, A.H.Q. India, 23/9/11-31/3/16; G.S.O.1, India, 20/12/18-18/12/19; G.S.O.1, India, 5/7/20-30/11/20.

N.W. Frontier, Waziristan, 1901-02; N.W. Frontier, 1903-04; N.W. Frontier, 1908 (wounded); War of 1914-18, despatches twice, D.S.O., French Croix de Guerre; Afghanistan, 1919, Bt. Lieut.-Colonel.

FINNIS, J. Ensign, Indian Army, 12/12/57. Ensign, 5th European Infantry, 18/5/58; Lieutenant, 18/11/60; Captain, 12/12/69; Major, 12/12/77. Posted to 5th P.I., 6/7/83; Lieut.-Colonel, 12/12/83. Died at Mussoorie, 12/9/84.

Mutiny Campaign, 1857-58.

FLOOD, J. D. M. 2nd-Lieutenant, Royal Irish Fusiliers, 23/4/02. Appointed to Bombay S.C., 26/1/04. Posted to 58th, 27/5/04; Lieutenant, 23/7/04; Captain, 26/5/09; Major, 1/9/15; Bt. Lieut.-Colonel, 3/6/19; Bt. Colonel, 3/6/23; Lieut.-Colonel, 27/8/24; G.S.O.2, India, 16/8/19-15/9/19. D.A.Q.M.G., Waziristan, 11/10/19-10/1/20.

South African War, 1901-02; War of 1914-18, despatches, Bt. Lieut.-Colonel; Waziristan, 1919-21, despatches.

FOSTER, R. 2nd-Lieutenant, Unattached List, 8/5/01. Appointed to Bengal S.C., 6/11/02; Lieutenant, 8/8/03. Posted to 58th, 21/3/04. Joined Survey Dept.; Captain, 8/5/10; Major, 8/5/16.

War of 1914-18, N.W. Frontier.

FOWLER, E. K. 2nd-Lieutenant, The Wiltshire Regiment, 29/8/06; Lieutenant, 29/11/08. Appointed to Indian Army, 19/3/09; Captain, 29/8/15; Bt. Major, 1/1/18; Major, 29/8/21; D.A.A.G., Southern Command, India, 4/4/24.

War of 1914-18: Belgium, East Africa, despatches, Bt. Major, Military Cross; Afghanistan, 1919; Waziristan, 1919.

FROST, R. L. 2nd-Lieutenant, Unattached List, 30/1/17. Appointed to Indian Army, 15/2/17. Posted to 58th, 21/12/17; Lieutenant, 30/1/18; Captain, 30/1/21.

GAISFORD, G. Ensign, Indian Army, 22/2/68, and posted same date to 11th Bengal N.I.; Lieutenant, 23/3/70. Posted to 5th P.I., 2/6/71; Captain, 22/2/80; Major, 22/2/88; Lieut.-Colonel, 22/3/94; murdered near Dukhi, Baluchistan, 15/3/98, when employed as Political Agent.

N.W. Frontier, 1877-78, despatches; Afghan War, 1878-80, despatches; N.W. Frontier, despatches.

GAISFORD, L. 2nd-Lieutenant, Unattached List, 29/8/06. Appointed to Indian Army, 20/10/07.

War of 1914-18, killed in action, 23/11/14.

GALBRAITH, E. D. 2nd-Lieutenant, The East Lancashire Regiment, 19/6/01; Lieutenant, 9/6/04. Appointed to Indian Army, same date; Captain 19/6/10; Major, 19/6/16; Lieut.-Colonel, 1/2/26; Staff Captain, War Office, 1/11/14-21/8/15; D.A.A.G., France, 22/8/15-8/12/15; D.A.A. & Q.M.G., France, 9/12/15-22/5/17; D.A.Q.M.G., India, 19/4/19-31/10/20; D.A.A.G., 1/11/20-8/6/22.

N.W. Frontier, 1897; War of 1914-18, despatches, twice, Bt. Major, D.S.O., Legion of Honour.

GARROW, R. K. 2nd-Lieutenant, Unattached List, 1/10/18. Appointed to Indian Army, 13/10/18; Lieutenant, 1/10/19. Posted to 58th same date; Captain, 1/10/24.

GASTRELL, J. E. Ensign, Indian Army, 11/2/35. Posted to 13th Bengal N.I., 12/9/36; Lieutenant, 8/10/39; Captain, 13/3/49. Appointed Commandant 5th P.I. on raising of the Regiment, 18/4/49. Appointed to Survey Dept., 13/1/52; Major, 24/3/58; Lieut.-Colonel, 18/2/63; Colonel, 11/12/66; Dep. Surveyor General, 11/3/67; Major-General, 11/10/77; Lieut.-General, 1/7/81; General, 22/1/89; died at Bedford, 29/8/94.

Jeypore Campaign, 1838; Bundelkhand, 1842-43; Punjab War, 1848-49; Sonthal Campaign, 1855.

GILLESPIE, D. S. Lieutenant, Indian Army, 4/1/16. Posted to 58th, 11/5/17; Captain, 20/10/19.

War of 1914-18: Gallipoli, Egypt, France and Belgium, Egyptian Expeditionary Force, despatches.

GORDON, S. Lieutenant, I.M.S., 27/7/12. Posted to 58th, 5/4/14; Captain, 27/7/15; Major, 27/7/24.

War of 1914-18, despatches twice, Military Cross.

GRAY, F. W. B. 2nd-Lieutenant, The Berkshire Regiment, 22/8/88; Lieutenant, Madras S.C., 22/1/90; Captain, 22/8/99; Posted to 58th, 26/4/05; Major, 22/8/06; Lieut.-Colonel, 8/3/14; Temp. Brig.-General, 15/4/16-27/11/17; Bt. Colonel, 1/1/18; Brigade Commander, Egyptian Expeditionary Force, 15/4/16-27/11/17; Brigade Commander, India, 13/5/18; retired with rank of Brig.-General in 1921.

N.W. Frontier, 1894-95; China Expeditionary Force, 1900; N.W. Frontier, 1908, despatches, D.S.O.; War of 1914-18, despatches, three times, Bt. Colonel, C.M.G.

GREEN, G. W. G. Ensign, Indian Army, 12/6/41; Ensign, 2nd European Regt., 6/11/41; Lieutenant, 26/8/43. Posted as Second-in-Command 5th P.I. on raising of the Regiment, 18/5/49. Appointed Commandant 2nd P.I., 18/10/52; Captain, 24/11/53; Major, 19/1/58; Bt. Lieut.-Colonel, 24/3/58; Bt. Colonel, 22/9/63; Major-General, 30/3/69; Awarded K.C.B., 2/6/77; Lieut.-General, 1/10/77; retired with rank of General, 11/6/79; died at Cheltenham, 27/11/91.

Scinde, 1845; Punjab War, 1848-49; N.W. Frontier, 1855; N.W. Frontier, 1857; Indian Mutiny Campaign, 1857-58 (wounded), Bt. Major and Bt. Lieut.-Colonel; awarded C.B.; N.W. Frontier, 1860.

HALL, C. McK. Ensign, Indian Army, 20/12/60; Lieutenant, 7/1/62. Posted to 5th P.I., 16/8/65; Captain, 1/1/70; Major, 20/12/80; Lieut.-Colonel, 20/12/86; retired, 5/8/87; died at Tunbridge Wells in 1896.

Ambela Expedition, 1863; Afghan War, 1878-80, despatches; N.W. Frontier, 1881, despatches.

HAYLEY, H. Ensign, Indian Army, 27/7/44. Posted to 69th Bengal N.I., 13/2/45; Lieutenant, 31/7/49; Captain, 27/7/59; Appointed Dep. Inspr. of Police, Kohat, 4/6/63; Major, 27/7/64; died, 19/3/65.

HOLGATE, M. J. Lieutenant, I.M.S., 31/7/09; Captain, 31/7/12. Posted to 58th, 1916; Major, 31/1/21.

War of 1914-18: Egyptian Expeditionary Force, despatches, O.B.E.

HOLLAND, P. Lieutenant, The Duke of Cornwall's L.I., 22/10/81; Appointed Indian Staff Corps same date. Posted to 5th Bombay Infantry as Quartermaster, 1/8/84. Posted to 5th P.I., 30/9/87; Captain, 22/10/92; Major, 29/11/00; Lieut.-Colonel, 1/6/04; Colonel, 11/6/07; retired, 12/10/13.

Egyptian Expedition, 1882; Burma War, 1885-1887, despatches, twice; N.W. Frontier, 1891; N.W. Frontier, 1897-98; South African War, 1899-00; China Expedition, 1900.

ILLIUS, H. W. Lieutenant, I.M.S., 27/6/01. Posted to 5th P.I., 8/5/02; Captain, 27/6/04; Major, 27/12/12; Lieut.-Colonel, 27/12/20

N.W. Frontier, Waziristan, 1901-02; Tibet, 1903-04; War of 1914-18, despatches; Mesopotamia, 1920, despatches; Awarded C.I.E.

JACKSON, H. J. R. 2nd-Lieutenant, Unattached List, 18/4/16. Posted to 58th, 25/4/16; Lieutenant, 18/1/17; Captain, 18/4/20.

War of 1914-18, despatches.

JAMES, F. P. 2nd-Lieutenant, The East Surrey Regiment, 18/2/91; Lieutenant, 1/2/93. Appointed to Bengal S.C., 11/5/93. Posted to 5th P.I., 4/12/95; Captain, 10/7/01; retired, 20/5/09; N.W. Frontier, 1897-98.

JAMESON, R. F. Ensign, 25th Foot, 28/10/71; Lieutenant same date; Appointed to Indian Staff Corps, 31/7/74 and posted to 5th P.I.; Captain, 28/10/83; Major, 28/10/91; Bt. Lieut.-Colonel, 6/11/95; Commandant, 5th P.I., 16/4/94; Lieut.-Colonel, 29/10/97; retired, 19/2/06.

Afghan War, 1878-80; N.W. Frontier, 1881.

JAMIESON, J. W. E. 2nd-Lieutenant, I.A.R.O., 8/1/15. Posted to 58th, 16/8/15; Lieutenant, 8/10/16. Appointed to Indian Army, 4/6/17; Captain, 8/10/19.

JENKINS, F. H. Ensign, Indian Army, 20/12/51. Posted to 57th Bengal N.I., 17/11/52; Lieutenant, 15/11/53; Captain, 1/1/62; Commandant, 5th P.I., 11/3/69; Major, 20/12/70; Lieut.-Colonel, 20/12/77. Awarded C.B., 25/7/79; Colonel, 29/10/79; A.D.C. to the Queen; retired, 15/7/85.
Mutiny Campaign, 1857-58 (severely wounded); N.W. Frontier, 1859; N.W. Frontier, 1860; N.W. Frontier, Ambela, 1863; N.W. Frontier, 1878.

JENKINS, J. S. 2nd-Lieutenant, Unattached List, 15/4/19. Appointed to Indian Army, 22/4/19; Lieutenant, 15/4/20; Captain, 15/4/25.
N.W. Frontier, Waziristan, 1921, despatches.

JOHNSON, G. W. 2nd-Lieutenant, King's Own Scottish Borderers, 14/9/87; Lieutenant, 28/1/89. Posted to 3rd P.C. same date; Captain, 14/9/98; Posted to 5th P.I., 22/5/02; Major, 14/9/05. Posted to 47th Sikhs, 30/4/06; Lieut.-Colonel, 14/9/13.
Burma War, 1887.

JOHNSTON, J. C. Ensign, Indian Army, 2/2/35. Posted to 29th Bengal Infantry, 24/9/35; Lieutenant, 3/2/39; Commandant, 2nd P.I., 18/5/49; Captain, 21/12/49; Commandant, 1st Sikhs, 23/11/50; Commandant, 5th P.I., 5/11/51; retired, 27/8/53.

JOHNSTONE, A. A. J. 2nd-Lieutenant, The Leinster Regiment, 22/1/81; Lieutenant, Indian S.C., 1/7/81. Posted to 5th P.I., 10/4/85; Captain 22/1/92; Major, 22/1/01; Commandant, 58th, 15/5/04; Lieut.-Colonel, 1/6/04; Bt. Colonel, 11/6/07; retired, with rank of Brig.-General, 19/2/06. Appointed Hon. Colonel, 58th, 1/2/21.
Afghan War, 1878-80; N.W. Frontier, 1881.

JOLLY, G. G. Lieutenant, I.M.S., 1/8/08. Posted to 58th, 8/7/11; Captain, 1/8/11; Major, 1/2/20.
War of 1914-18, East Africa, C.I.E.

KITSON, R. B. 2nd-Lieutenant, Unattached List, 13/8/04. Appointed to Indian Army, 29/10/05; Lieutenant, 13/11/06. Posted to 58th, 22/2/08; Captain, 13/8/13; killed in action, 13/11/17.
War of 1914-18.

KNOLLYS, R. W. E. 2nd-Lieutenant, Unattached List, 23/1/93. Appointed to Madras S.C., 28/3/94. Posted to 5th P.I., 8/7/94; Lieutenant, 28/4/95. Appointed Adjutant, 2/9/97. Appointed to Civil Dept., Punjab, 17/1/01; Captain, 28/1/02; Major, 28/1/11; Lieut.-Colonel, 28/1/19.
N.W. Frontier, 1897-98.

KNOX, A. W. F. 2nd-Lieutenant, The Royal Irish Rifles, 2/5/91; Lieutenant, Indian S.C., 18/11/93. Posted to 5th P.I., 30/5/98; Captain, 2/5/02; Major, 2/5/09; Bt. Lieut.-Colonel, 24/7/15; Bt. Colonel, 1/1/17; Major-General, 9/7/18; retired, 24/7/20; M.P. for Bucks since 30/10/24;

A.D.C. Viceroy, India, December, 1899, to March, 1900 ; A.D.C. Viceroy, India, April, 1902, to March, 1903 ; G.S.O. War Office, January, 1908, to May, 1911 ; Military Attaché, Petrograd, and Liaison Officer, Russian Army, 2/5/11-16/1/18 ; Chief of British Mission, Siberia, 16/7/18 to December, 1919.

N.W. Frontier, 1901-02, despatches ; War of 1914-18 ; C.M.G., 1918 ; K.C.B., 1919 ; Orders of St. Stanislaus, St. Vladimir, St. Anne ; Comdr. Legion of Honour, Croix de Guerre ; Crown of Italy ; Croix de Guerre, Czecho-Slovakia ; Rising Sun of Japan.

LAWRENCE, H. R. 2nd-Lieutenant, Royal Artillery, 28/3/00 ; Lieutenant, 3/4/01. Appointed to Bengal S.C., 13/4/03. Posted to 58th, 27/10/03 ; Political Employ, 9/4/04 ; Captain, 23/3/09 ; Major, 1/9/15 ; Lieut.-Colonel, 28/3/26.

War of 1914-18, despatches ; C.I.E.

LEE, J. L. 2nd-Lieutenant, Unattached List, 17/12/19. Appointed to Indian Army, 19/4/20 ; Lieutenant, 17/12/20.

LIND, A. G. 2nd-Lieutenant, York and Lancaster Regiment, 1/12/97 ; Lieutenant, 4/4/00 ; Bombay S.C., 16/9/00. Posted to 5th P.I., 29/9/00 ; Captain, 1/12/06 ; Major, 1/12/15 ; Commandant 5th P.I., 1/2/21 ; Lieut.-Colonel, 1/2/21 ; Colonel, 1/2/25 ; retired, 26/9/26.

War of 1914-18 : France and Belgium, Egypt, Egyptian Expeditionary Force, despatches twice, (wounded) ; D.S.O. ; French Croix de Guerre ; Waziristan, 1920-21, despatches.

LIND, J. B. Ensign, Indian Army, 26/5/46. Posted to 24th Bengal N.I., 1/2/47 ; Lieutenant, 18/11/50. Appointed Adjutant 5th P.I., 10/11/53 ; Captain, 16/2/61. To 31st Foot in 1862 ; Bt. Major, 19/1/64 ; retired, 7/1/74, with rank of Colonel.

N.W. Frontier, 1856 ; Mutiny Campaign, 1857-58, raised and commanded Lind's Multani Horse (twice wounded, and five horses killed or wounded under him), thanks of Government, several times mentioned in despatches, Bt. Major.

LLOYD, R. B. Lieutenant, I.M.S., 1/8/08. Posted to 58th, 15/11/10 ; Captain, 1/8/11 ; Major, 1/2/20.

War of 1914-18, despatches.

LOCH, W. Appointed Ensign, 36th Bengal N.I., 4/1/62 ; Lieutenant, 13/3/63. Posted to 5th P.I., 22/6/64. Posted to 19th Lancers, I.A., 1/3/65 ; Captain, 18/7/71 ; A.D.C. Viceroy, India, 8/11/76 ; Major, 1/7/81 ; Lieut.-Colonel, 4/1/88 ; retired, 20/8/00.

N.W. Frontier, Ambela, 1863-64.

McCONKEY, A. I. G. 2nd-Lieutenant, Unattached List, 13/1/14 ; Lieutenant, 1/9/15. Appointed to Indian Army, 12/9/15. Posted to 58th, 7/11/15 ; Captain, 13/1/18 ; Staff Captain, India, 24/10/21.

War of 1914-18 : France and Belgium (wounded), Egyptian Expeditionary Force (wounded) ; N.W. Frontier, 1921.

MACKENZIE, A. W. Surgeon, I.M.S., 31/3/77. Posted to 5th P.I., 13/12/81; Surgeon-Major, 31/3/89. Posted to 5th Gurkhas, 20/1/96.

MACKENZIE, D. B. 2nd-Lieutenant, Unattached List, 21/1/13; Lieutenant, 21/4/15. Appointed to Indian Army, 28/8/15. Posted to 58th, 12/11/15; Captain, 21/1/17.

War of 1914-18, despatches.

MACKERTICH, S. Assistant-Surgeon, I.M.S., 1/10/60. Posted to 5th P.I., 20/12/64; Surgeon-Major, 1/10/72; retired, 6/9/81; died, 17/10/81.

MCNEILE, W. Ensign, Indian Army, 25/1/41. Posted to 5th European Infantry, 12/11/42; Lieutenant, 8/7/48. Posted as Adjutant to 5th P.I. on raising of Regiment, 18/5/49; Captain, 25/1/56. To Civil Employ, 15/6/59; Major, 18/2/61; Lieut.-Colonel, 25/1/67. Awarded C.S.I.; died at Amritsar, 25/5/70.

MCQUEEN, J. W. Ensign, Indian Army, 4/4/54. Posted to 27th Bengal N.I., 20/10/54; Lieutenant, 4/6/57. Posted to 4th P.I., 3/4/60; Captain, 4/4/66; Commandant 5th P.I., 10/6/70; Major, 4/4/74. Awarded C.B., 19/11/79; Lieut.-Colonel, 22/11/79; Colonel, 31/12/81; Major-General 10/12/92; Lieut.-General, 29/10/95; retired, 8/11/97; Hon. Colonel, 57th, 13/5/04; G.C.B., 29/6/06; died, 15/8/09.

Indian Mutiny, 1857-58 (wounded twice), despatches; N.W. Frontier, 1860; N.W. Frontier, 1869; N.W. Frontier, Jawaki, 1877-78, despatches; Afghan War, 1878-80, despatches; Bt. Lieut.-Colonel, C.B.; N.W. Frontier, 1881, despatches; N.W. Frontier, 1888, thanks of Government, K.C.B.

MANLOVE, J. E. D. 2nd-Lieutenant, The Royal Lancaster Regiment, 17/6/15; Lieutenant, 17/6/16. Posted to 58th, 31/7/18. Appointed to Indian Army, 12/1/19; Captain, 17/6/19.

MEIN, F. B. 2nd-Lieutenant, 84th Foot, 11/5/78; 2nd-Lieutenant, 63rd Foot, 27/9/79; Lieutenant, 1/7/81. Appointed to Bengal S.C., 5/7/83; Captain, 11/5/89. Posted to 5th P.I., 1/4/82; Major, 11/5/98; Commandant, 12th B.I., 14/6/90; died, 29/3/03.

Afghan War, 1878-80; N.W. Frontier, 1897-98.

MEIN, J. E. Ensign, 96th Foot, 6/7/70; Lieutenant, 28/10/71. Appointed to Bengal S.C., 15/7/73, and posted to 5th P.I. same date; Captain, 6/7/82. Posted to 6th P.I., 29/5/87; Major, 6/7/90; Lieut.-Colonel, 6/7/96; Colonel, 6/7/00; retired, 15/9/08.

N.W. Frontier, Jawaki, 1877-78; Afghan War, 1878-80; N.W. Frontier, 1881; N.W. Frontier, 1891; N.W. Frontier, 1894-95.

MILLIGAN, J. H. 2nd-Lieutenant, The Connaught Rangers, 4/5/07; Lieutenant, 4/8/09. Appointed to Indian Army, 26/10/09. Posted to 58th same date; killed in action, 25/9/15.

War of 1914-18.

MONEY, G. N. Ensign, Indian Army, 4/3/53. Posted 2nd-Lieutenant, 1st European Fusiliers, 6/9/53; Lieutenant, 5/3/56. Posted to 3rd P.I., 22/2/64; Captain, 4/3/65. Posted to 5th P.I., 25/11/68; Major, 4/3/73. Posted to 3rd Sikhs, 27/3/73; Lieut.-Colonel, 4/3/79; retired, 1/7/82.

Burma War, 1853-54; Mutiny Campaign, 1857-58; N.W. Frontier, Ambela, 1863; N.W. Frontier, Jawaki, 1877-78, despatches.

MUNRO, D. Lieutenant, I.M.S., 29/1/02. Posted to 58th, 12/3/04; Captain, 29/1/05. To Civil Employ same year.

NEWMAN, E. A. R. Lieutenant, I.M.S., 29/7/93; Captain, 29/7/96; Major, 29/7/05; Lieut.-Colonel, 30/1/13; retired, 29/1/23.
N.W. Frontier, 1897-98.

NICOLLS, J. O. 2nd-Lieutenant, Unattached List, 2/9/08. Appointed to Indian Army, 11/12/09. Posted to 58th same date; Lieutenant, 9/12/10; killed in action, 25/9/15.
War of 1914-18.

NOLAN, L. McN. 2nd-Lieutenant, Unattached List, 15/4/19; Lieutenant same date. Posted to 58th, 18/4/19. Appointed to Indian Army, 19/4/19.

PALMER, C. E. Lieutenant, I.M.S., 1/9/05; Captain, 1/9/08. Posted to 58th, 29/9/08; Major, 5/11/15; Lieut.-Colonel, 1/3/25.

PARSONS, F. Assistant-Surgeon and posted to 3rd Bengal N.I., 10/2/59. Posted to 5th P.I., 23/5/62 Posted to 2nd B.C., 12/12/70; Surgeon-Major, 10/2/71.

PEARSON, G. T. 2nd-Lieutenant, Unattached List, 27/10/17. Posted to 58th, 3/11/17. Appointed to Indian Army, 4/11/17; Lieutenant, 27/11/17; Captain, 27/10/22.
N.W. Frontier, Afghanistan, 1919; N.W. Frontier, Waziristan, 1921.

PERRY, W. F. S. Appointed to Indian Army as Ensign, 22/11/59; Lieutenant, 10/8/61. Posted to 5th P.I., 28/6/65; Captain, 6/5/69; left the Service, 29/6/71.

POPE, S. B. 2nd-Lieutenant, Royal Irish Rifles, 4/5/01; Bombay Staff Corps, 8/4/03; Lieutenant, 4/8/03. Posted to 58th, 25/2/04; Captain, 10/5/10; Major, 4/5/16; Bt. Lieut.-Colonel, 1/1/19; Bt. Colonel, 3/5/21; G.S.O.3, France, 8/8/15-31/10/15; Brigade Major, France, 1/11/15-3/3/16; G.S.O.3, Egyptian Expeditionary Force, 27/5/16-3/8/16; G.S.O.1, India, 29/11/19-30/6/22; D.A.A. & Q.M.G., India, 1/7/22-31/7/23.

N.W. Frontier, 1908; War of 1914-18, France, Belgium, Egyptian Expeditionary Force, despatches four times, Bt. Lieut.-Colonel, D.S.O., Legion of Honour, Order of the Nile.

RATNAGAR, S. D. Lieutenant, I.M.S., 27/7/12. Posted to 58th, 14/8/13. To Civil Employ in 1914.

READ, A. W. C. Ensign, 51st Foot, 15/5/55; Lieutenant, 17/11/57. Appointed to Indian Army same date. Posted as Adjutant to 5th P.I., 1/3/64; Captain, 15/5/67; died at Netley, 5/5/74.

REEVE, M. B. P. 2nd-Lieutenant, Unattached List, 18/6/17. Appointed to Indian Army, 14/7/17; Lieutenant, 18/6/18. Posted to 58th, 5/6/19; Captain, 18/6/21.

War of 1914-18; N.W. Frontier, Egyptian Expeditionary Force.

REINHOLD, C. H. Lieutenant, I.M.S., 1/9/05. Posted to 58th, 26/4/08; Captain, 1/9/08; Major, 15/11/15; Lieut.-Colonel, 1/3/25.

ROSS-HURST, W. J. O'B. 2nd-Lieutenant, Unattached List, 29/6/16. Appointed to Indian Army and posted to 58th, 29/7/16; Lieutenant, 29/6/17; Captain, 29/6/20.

ROUSE, R. Assistant-Surgeon, I.M.S., 20/11/54. Posted to 5th P.I., 9/5/56. Posted to 5th P.C., 22/1/58; Surgeon-Major, 20/12/66. Posted to 3rd P.C., 19/2/68. To Civil Employ in 1875.

RUSSELL, W. R. 2nd-Lieutenant, Unattached List, 29/1/20. Posted to 58th, 5/2/20. Appointed to Indian Army, 6/2/20; Lieutenant, 29/1/21.

SCOTT, T. E. 2nd-Lieutenant, Royal Irish Fusiliers, 9/5/88; Lieutenant, 18/12/89. Appointed to Bengal S.C., 17/4/90; Captain, 9/5/99; Bt. Major, 10/5/99; Major, 13/2/05. Posted to 58th, 15/5/11; Lieut.-Colonel, 10/5/12; Colonel, 29/11/15; Major-General, 3/6/18; Colonel Royal Irish Fusiliers, 20/11/23; Lieut.-General, 14/2/24; Mil. Sec. to C.-in-C., India, 1/1/18-15/11/19; Brigade Commander, India, 16/11/19-18/2/25. Awarded D.S.O., 1897; C.I.E., 1900; K.C.B., 1925; Rising Sun of Japan; Brilliant Star of Zanzibar.

N.W. Frontier, 1891; N.W. Frontier, 1894-95; East Africa, 1896; Uganda, 1897-98, Bt. Major; China, 1900, despatches, twice; War of 1914-18, despatches.

SHEPHERD, A. I. Ensign, 93rd Highlanders, 20/12/61; Lieutenant, 30/6/68. Posted to 4th P.I. as Adjutant, 21/12/71; Captain, 20/12/73; Major, 20/12/81. Posted to 5th P.I., 8/11/84; died at Abbottabad, 7/12/84.
N.W. Frontier, Jawaki, 1877.

SLATER, D. McL. 2nd-Lieutenant, Royal Scots Fusiliers, 18/1/02; Lieutenant, Indian Army, and posted to 5th P.I., 9/5/05; Captain, 18/1/11; Major, 18/1/17.

War of 1914-18: East Africa, N.W. Frontier, despatches, Legion of Honour.

SMALLEY, J. B. 2nd-Lieutenant, The Gloucestershire Regiment, 20/9/11; Lieutenant, 15/10/13; Captain, 20/9/15. Appointed to Indian Army, 26/11/18.

SMITH, A. A. 2nd-Lieutenant, The East Lancashire Regt., 1/12/97; Lieutenant, 11/5/00. Appointed to Madras S.C., 8/2/01. Posted to 5th P.I., 18/10/01; Captain, 1/12/06; Major, 1/12/15; retired, 3/6/21.

N.W. Frontier, 1901-02; N.W. Frontier, 1908; War of 1914-18, despatches.

SMITH, P. W. Appointed Ensign, Indian Army, 8/6/61; Lieutenant, 15/12/62. Posted to 3rd Sikhs, 22/2/64. Posted to 5th P.I. as Quartermaster, 28/9/65; Captain, 30/3/70. Posted to Deoli Irregular Force, 23/1/80; Major, 8/6/81; Lieut.-Colonel, 8/6/87; Colonel, 29/9/93; retired, with rank of Major-General, 10/4/99.

N.W. Frontier, Ambela, 1863; Afghan War, 1878-80.

SOMERVILLE, M. R. Appointed Ensign, Indian Army, 12/6/41. Posted to 61st Bengal N.I., 13/11/41; Lieutenant, 25/1/43; Captain, 3/7/55. Posted to 5th P.I. as Second-in-Command, 3/4/60; died, 3/9/62.

SPEAR, C. R. 2nd-Lieutenant, Unattached List, 18/4/16. Appointed to Indian Army and posted to 58th, 25/4/16; Lieutenant, 18/4/17; Captain, 18/4/20.

War of 1914-18: Egyptian Expeditionary Force.

STEWART, C. E. Ensign, 27th Foot, 14/4/54; Lieutenant, 1/5/55. Appointed to Indian Army and posted to 5th P.I. as Adjutant, 13/4/58; Captain, 14/4/66; Major, 14/4/74; Lieut.-Colonel, 22/11/79; Commandant, 5th P.I., 6/1/83; Colonel, 22/11/83; C.M.G., 1884; C.I.E., 1884; C.B., 1886; retired, 23/2/93; Perso-Afghan Border, 1881-83 and 1884-85; Consul-General, Tabriz, 1889-92; Odessa, 1892-99; died, 26/12/04.

Mutiny Campaign, 1857-58, despatches, twice; N.W. Frontier, Ambela, 1863, despatches (wounded); N.W. Frontier, Jawaki, 1877, despatches, twice, Bt. Lieut.-Colonel.

STRETTELL, A. D. Ensign, General List, Bengal, 4/3/62; Lieutenant, 31/10/67; Bengal S.C., 18/11/69; Quartermaster, 2nd P.I., 2/6/71; Captain, 4/3/74; Major, 4/3/82; Lieut.-Colonel, 4/3/88; Commandant, 5th P.I., 27/7/90; retired, 16/4/94.

Abyssinian Campaign, 1868, despatches; Afghan War, 1878-80; N.W. Frontier, 1881; N.W. Frontier, Miranzai, 1891.

SUNDER, C. E. Surgeon-Captain, I.M.S., 31/3/87. Posted to 5th P.I., 1/7/90. To Civil Employ in 1895.

SUTTON, E. G. 2nd-Lieutenant, Unattached List, 16/7/20; Lieutenant, 16/7/21. Appointed to Indian Army, 22/11/21.

Waziristan, 1922-24.

THOMSON, A. G. 2nd-Lieutenant, Northamptonshire Regiment, 21/10/93; Lieutenant, 16/9/96. Appointed to Bombay S.C., 6/5/97. Posted to 5th P.I., 25/7/98; Captain, 21/10/02; Major, 21/10/11; Bt. Lieut.-Colonel, 3/6/18; retired, 2/5/20.

N.W. Frontier, 1902; War of 1914-18, despatches (wounded), Bt. Lieut.-Colonel, C.M.G., D.S.O., French and Belgian Croix de Guerre.

TIMS, E. D. 2nd-Lieutenant, Unattached List, 31/8/22. Appointed to Indian Army, 28/10/23 ; Lieutenant, 30/11/24.

VALLINGS, A. Ensign, Indian Army, 20/9/58 ; Lieutenant,, 41st Bengal N.I., 24/5/59. Posted as Adjutant to 1st P.I., 10/5/65; Captain, 20/9/70 ; Major, 20/9/78 ; Lieut.-Colonel, 20/9/84 ; Commandant, 5th P.I., 20/10/87; Colonel, 20/9/88 ; retired, 20/9/96.

Sikkim, 1861 ; N.W. Frontier, Ambela, 1863, despatches ; Afghan War, 1878-80 ; N.W. Frontier, 1881.

VAUGHAN, J. L. Ensign, Indian Army, 12/10/40. Posted to 21st Bengal N.I., 5/3/41 ; Lieutenant, 16/7/42 ; Captain, 30/6/50. Posted to 5th P.I., 5/11/51 ; Commandant, 5th P.I., 22/10/52 ; Major, 6/6/56 ; Lieut.-Colonel, 26/4/59 ; Colonel, 21/9/61 ; Major-General, 15/1/70 ; Lieut.-General, 1/10/77 ; retired, 1/7/82 ; General, 1/12/88. Appointed Hon. Colonel, 5th P.I., 13/5/04 ; died at Tunbridge Wells, 2/1/11.

Gwalior Campaign, 1843-44 ; Crimean War, 1854-56, Medjidieh ; N.W. Frontier, 1857 ; Mutiny Campaign, 1857-58, thanks of Government, Bt. Lieut.-Colonel ; N.W. Frontier, 1865, C.B. ; N.W. Frontier, 1868, despatches, K.C.B.

VENOUR, W. E. Lieutenant, 1st W. India Regiment, 2/8/85. Appointed to Bombay S.C., 13/12/88. Posted to 5th P.I., 18/7/90 ; Captain, 2/9/96 ; Major, 2/9/03 ; Commandant, 5th P.I., 15/5/11 ; Lieut.-Colonel, 15/5/11 ; killed in action, 31/10/14.

N.E. Frontier, 1889-90 ; N.W. Frontier, 1891 ; N.W. Frontier, 1897-98 (wounded) ; War of 1914-18.

WALLER, R. DE W. 2nd-Lieutenant, Royal Artillery, 23/7/01 ; Lieutenant, 23/10/03. Appointed to Indian Army, 22/5/09 ; Captain, 23/7/10 ; Major, 23/7/16 ; Lieut.-Colonel and Commandant 5th P.I., 16/2/26.

War of 1914-18 : France, Egyptian Expeditionary Force, despatches (wounded), D.S.O. ; N.W. Frontier, Waziristan, 1920-21, despatches, twice.

WATTS, J. B. 2nd-Lieutenant, South Staffordshire Regt., 4/5/01 ; Lieutenant same date. Appointed to Madras S.C., 27/4/03. Posted to 58th, 26/7/03. Posted to 4th Rajputs, 19/2/06 ; retired, 4/2/11.

WHITE, F. P. L. Sub-Lieutenant, 4th Dragoon Guards, 24/7/72 ; Lieutenant, 24/7/73 ; 72nd Highlanders, 6/10/75. Appointed to Bengal S.C., 2/5/79 ; Captain, 8/1/85. Posted to 5th P.I., 12/8/90 ; Major, 24/7/93 ; Lieut.-Colonel, 24/7/99 ; Commandant, 5th P.I., 18/4/01 ; Bt. Colonel, 10/2/04.

WILFORD, E. E. 2nd-Lieutenant, East Yorkshire Regt., 5/9/96 ; Lieutenant, 15/6/98. Appointed to Madras S.C., 19/12/98. Posted to 5th P.I., 19/12/00 ; Captain, 5/9/05 ; Major, 5/9/14 ; Lieut.-Colonel, 1/2/21.

War of 1914-18, despatches, D.S.O., O.B.E.

WILLIAMSON, J. Ensign, Indian Army, 8/1/42. Posted to 1st European L.I., 7/7/42; Lieutenant, 23/12/43. Posted as Adjutant to 5th P.I., 5/11/51; Second-in-Command, 18/10/53; Depy. Comm. Gen., Bengal, 18/11/53; Captain, 15/4/56; murdered by mutineers at Cawnpore, 27/6/57.

WILLIS, E. S. C. 2nd-Lieutenant, The Devonshire Regiment, 11/2/99; Lieutenant, 24/2/00. Appointed to Madras S.C., 10/12/03. Posted to 58th, 25/5/04; Captain, 11/2/08; Major, 1/9/15; Bt. Lieut.-Colonel, 3/6/19; Lieut.-Colonel, 1/2/21; Colonel, 14/2/24.

South African War, 1899-1901, despatches, D.S.O.; War of 1914-18: France and Belgium, Mesopotamia, Egyptian Expeditionary Force, despatches, Bt. Lieut.-Colonel; Waziristan, 1919-24, despatches, O.B.E.

YOUNG, C. Ensign, Indian Army, 4/12/60; Lieutenant, 1/1/62. Posted as Adjutant to Meywar Bhil Corps, 15/3/67; Captain, 27/11/69. Posted as Quartermaster to 5th P.I., 17/6/74; Major, 4/12/80; retired, 28/2/85.

N.W. Frontier, Jawaki, 1877-78; Afghan War, 1878-80 (wounded).

SKETCH to illustrate ENGAGEMENT of 23rd Nov. 1914.

Ⓐ = *The only communication trench leading to trenches held by the 58th Rifles & which was seized by the enemy.*

Ⓑ = *Machine Gun Redoubt on the right of the Centre Section manned by the 9th Bhopal Infantry*

Ⓒ = *Position occupied by Capt. Baldwin at 10·30 a.m. with two platoons Sikhs*

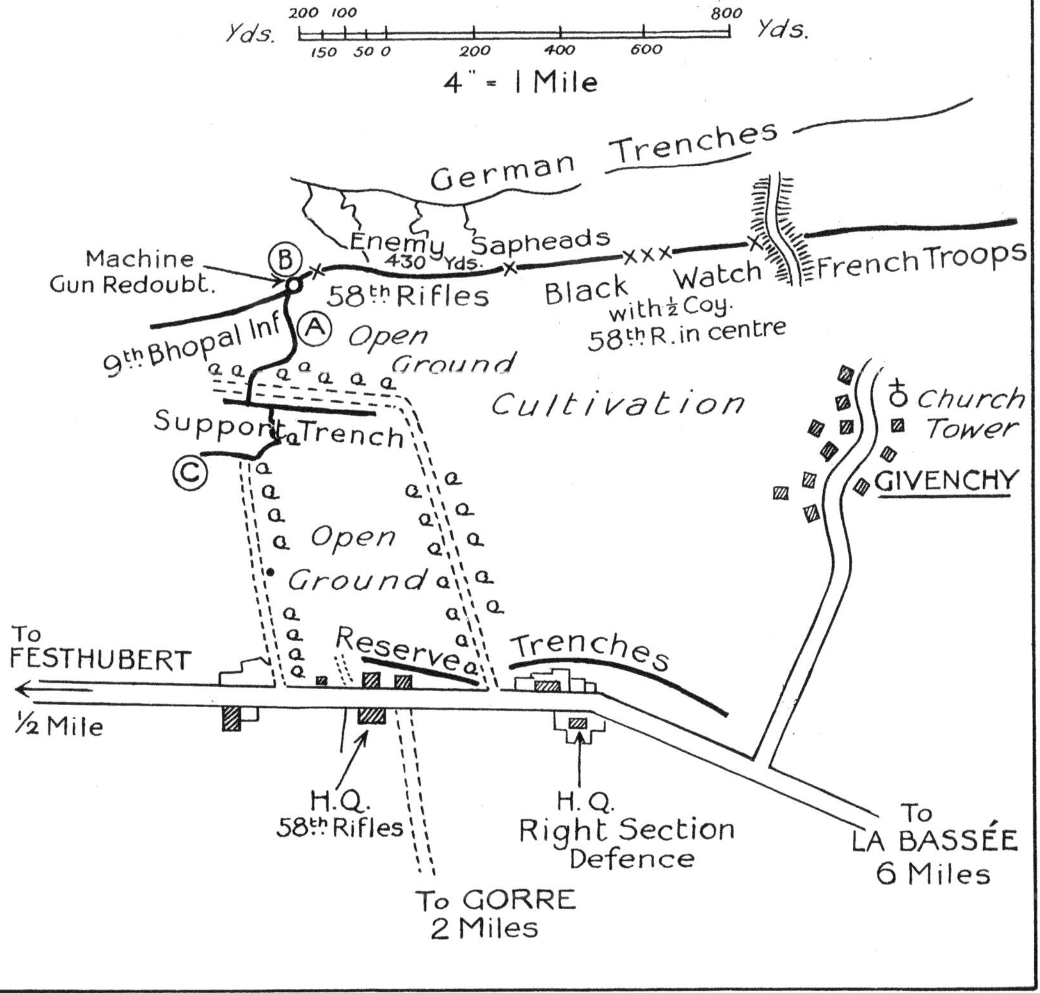

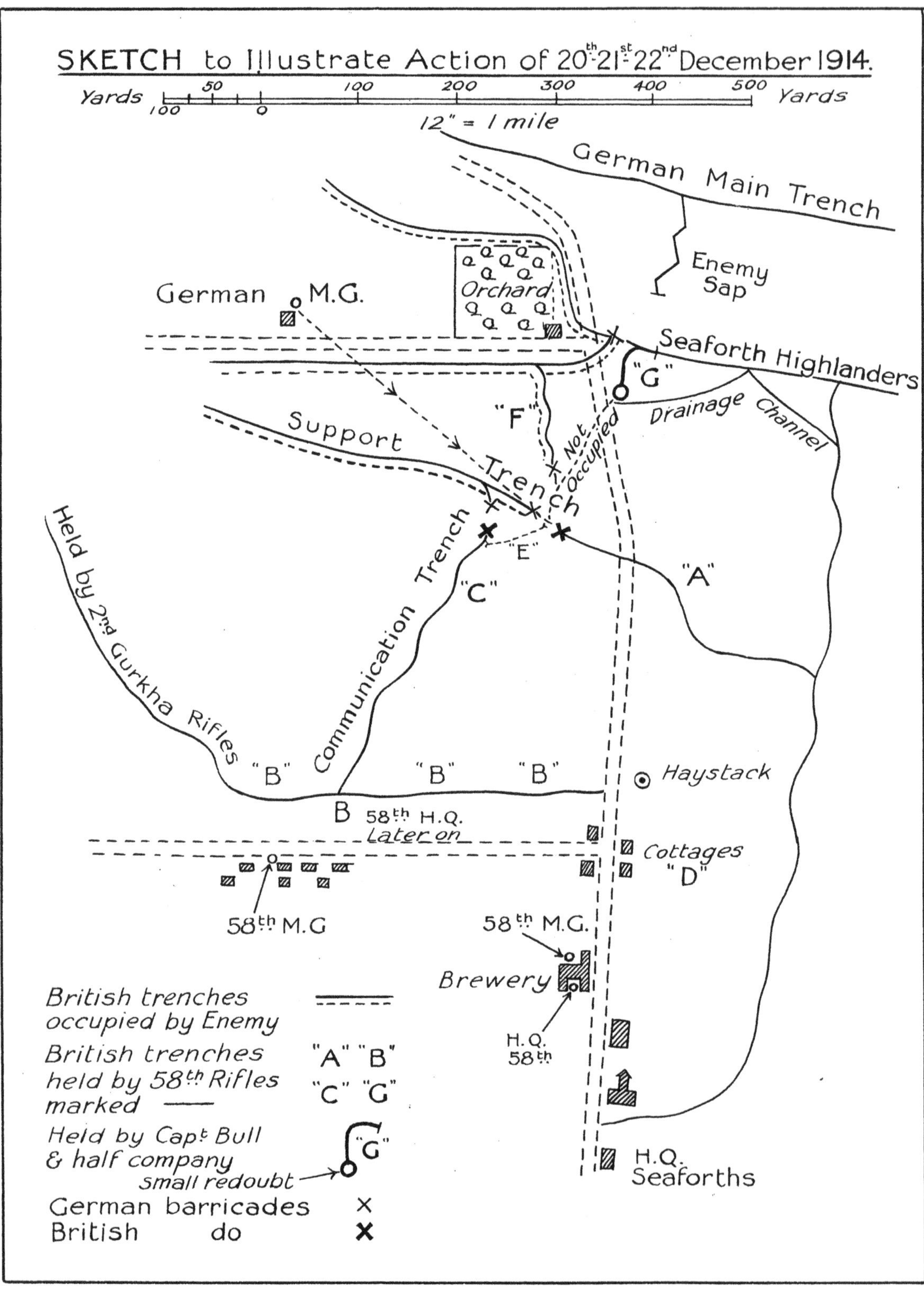
SKETCH to Illustrate Action of 20th 21st 22nd December 1914.
Yards 100 50 0 100 200 300 400 500 Yards
12" = 1 mile
German Main Trench
Enemy Sap
German M.G.
Orchard
Seaforth Highlanders
"G"
Drainage Channel
"F"
Not Occupied
Support Trench
Communication Trench
"E"
"C"
"A"
Held by 2nd Gurkha Rifles
"B" "B" "B"
B
58th H.Q. Later on
Haystack
Cottages "D"
58th M.G
58th M.G.
Brewery
H.Q. 58th
H.Q. Seaforths
British trenches occupied by Enemy
British trenches held by 58th Rifles marked
"A" "B" "C" "G"
Held by Capt Bull & half company small redoubt
"G"
German barricades ×
British do ✖

SKETCH TO ILLUSTRATE ACTION OF 25TH. SEPTEMBER, 1915

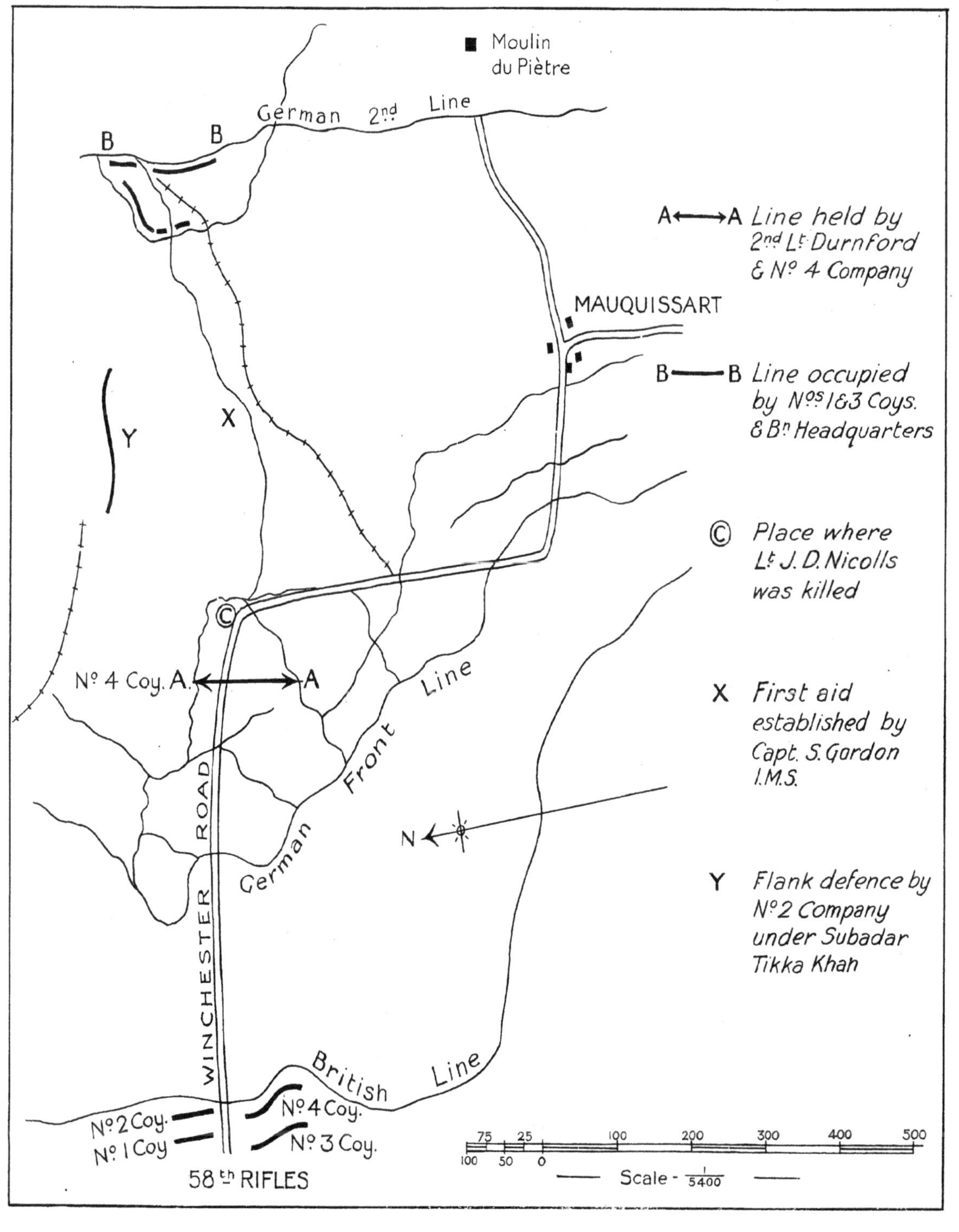

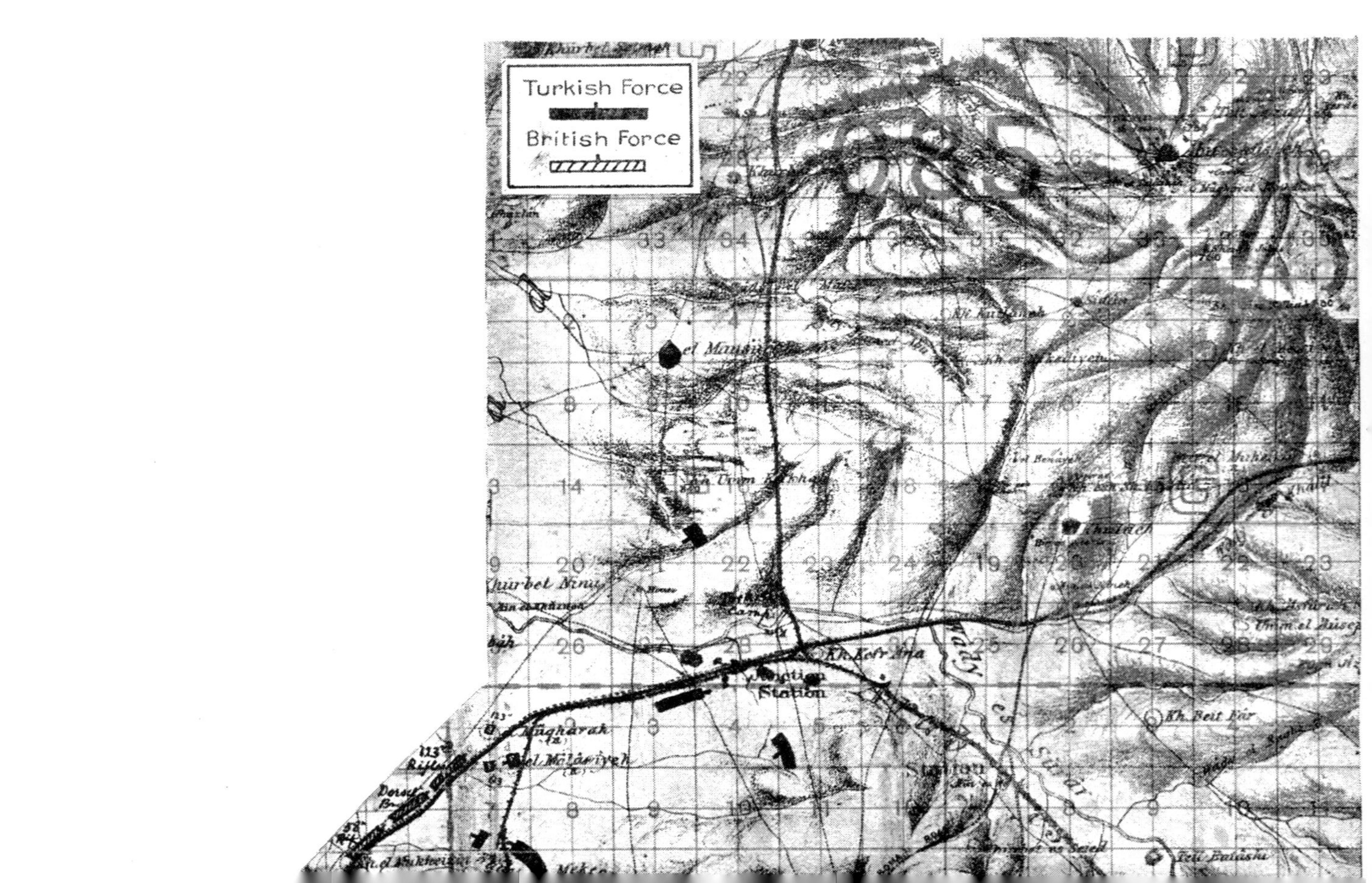
Turkish Force
British Force
Junction Station
Kh. Kefr Ana
Kh. Beit Far

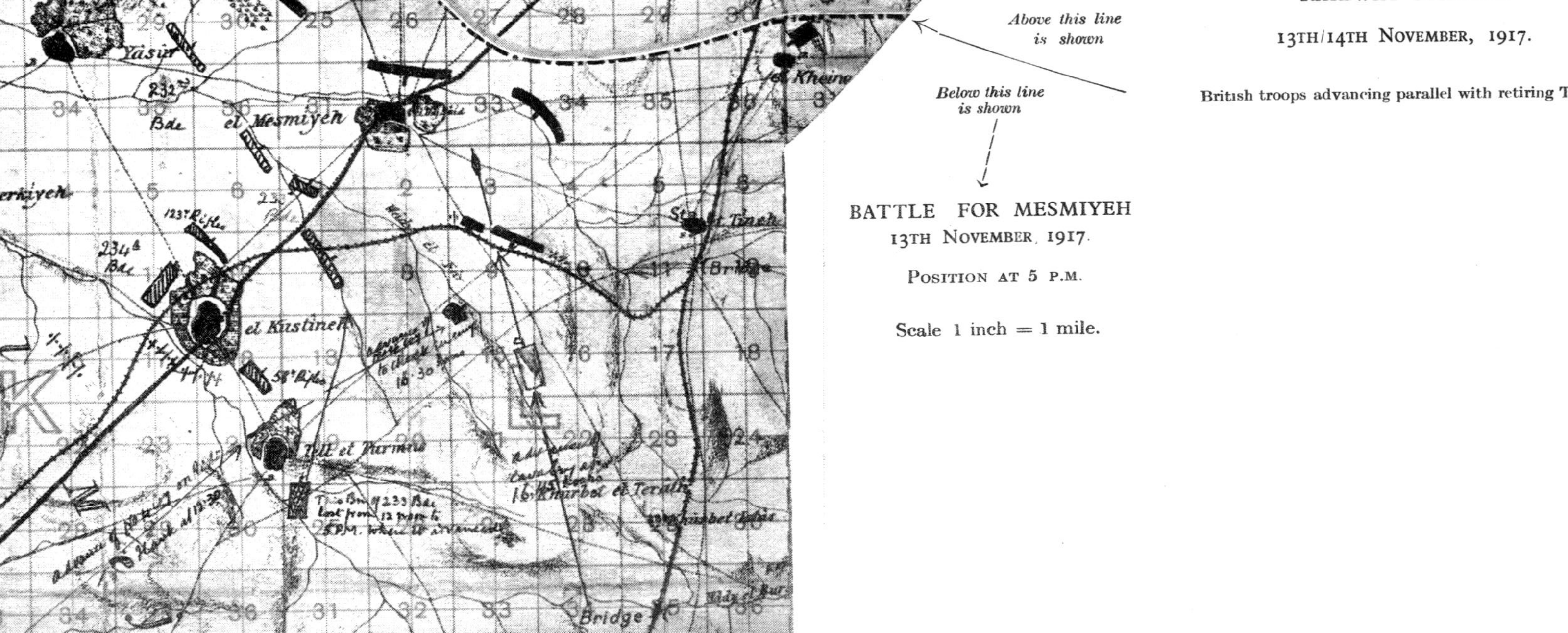

RAILWAY STATION

13TH/14TH NOVEMBER, 1917.

British troops advancing parallel with retiring Turks.

BATTLE FOR MESMIYEH

13TH NOVEMBER, 1917.

POSITION AT 5 P.M.

Scale 1 inch = 1 mile.

ACTION AT TABSOR (BATTLE OF SHARON)

19TH SEPTEMBER, 1918

SCALE $\frac{1}{40000}$: one inch = 1111 yards.

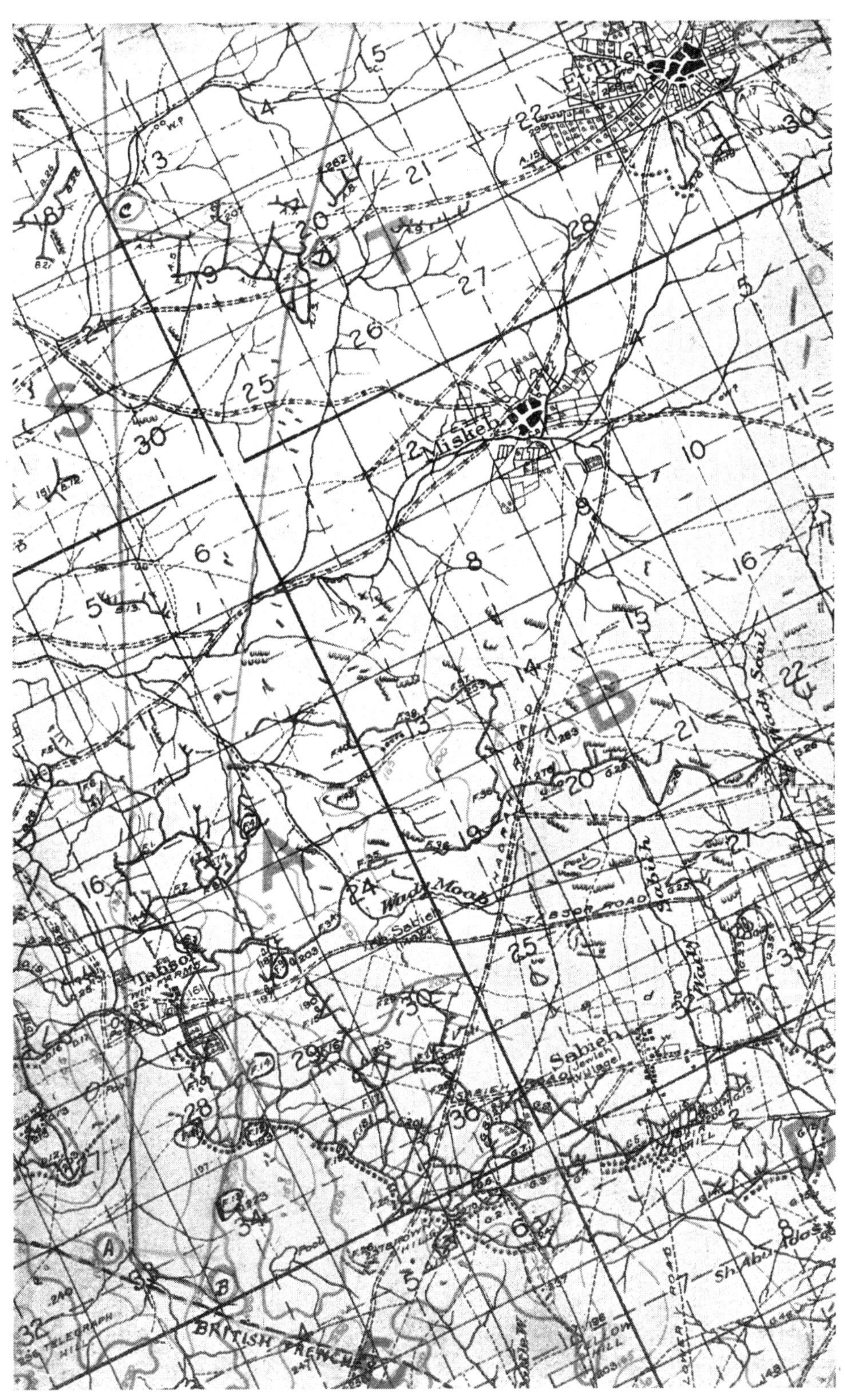

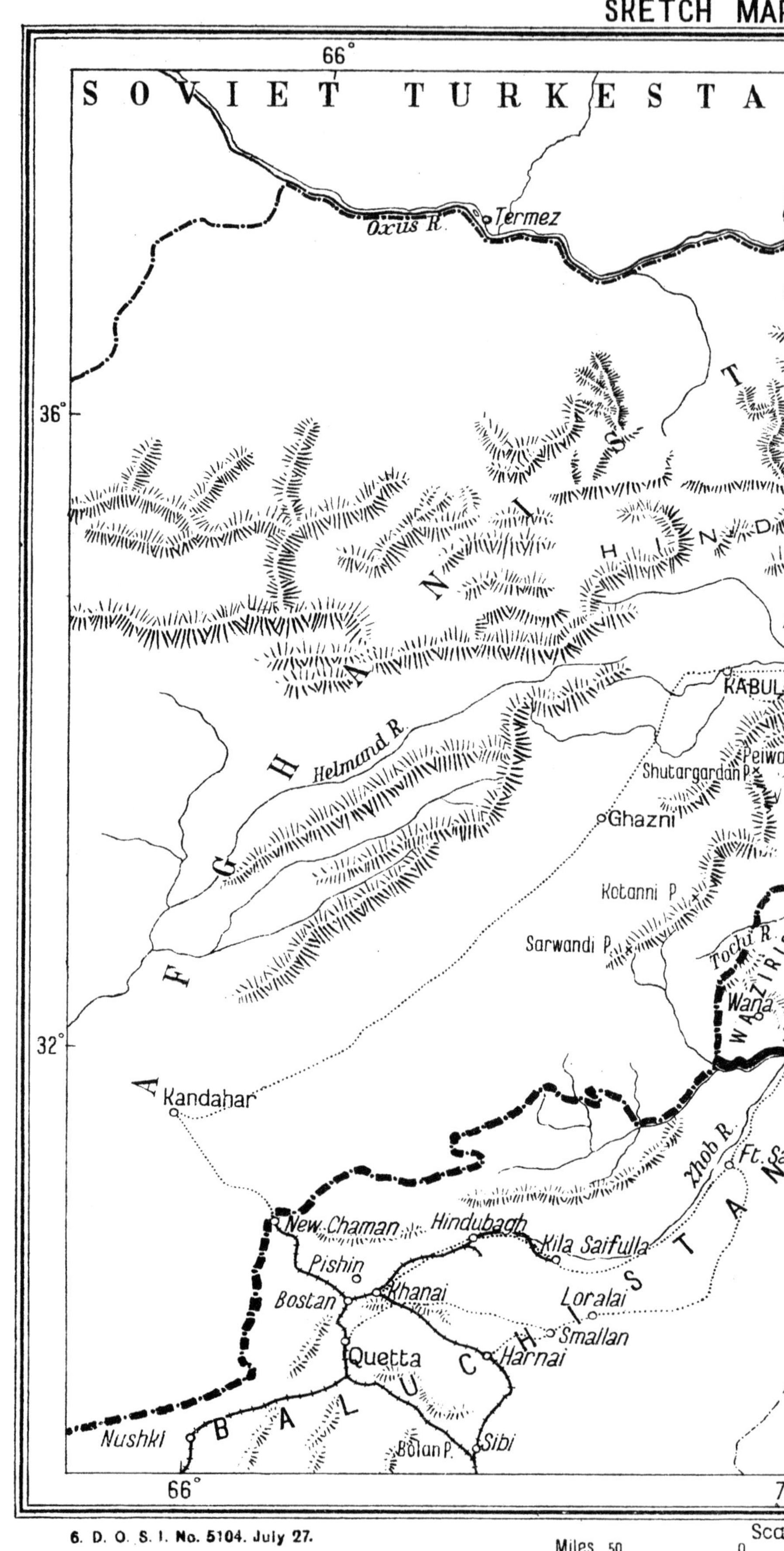

6. D. O. S. I. No. 5104. July 27.
Reg. No. 545 E.D.D. 1927-16,000-10,000.
" " 1928-20,000.

W. FRONTIER

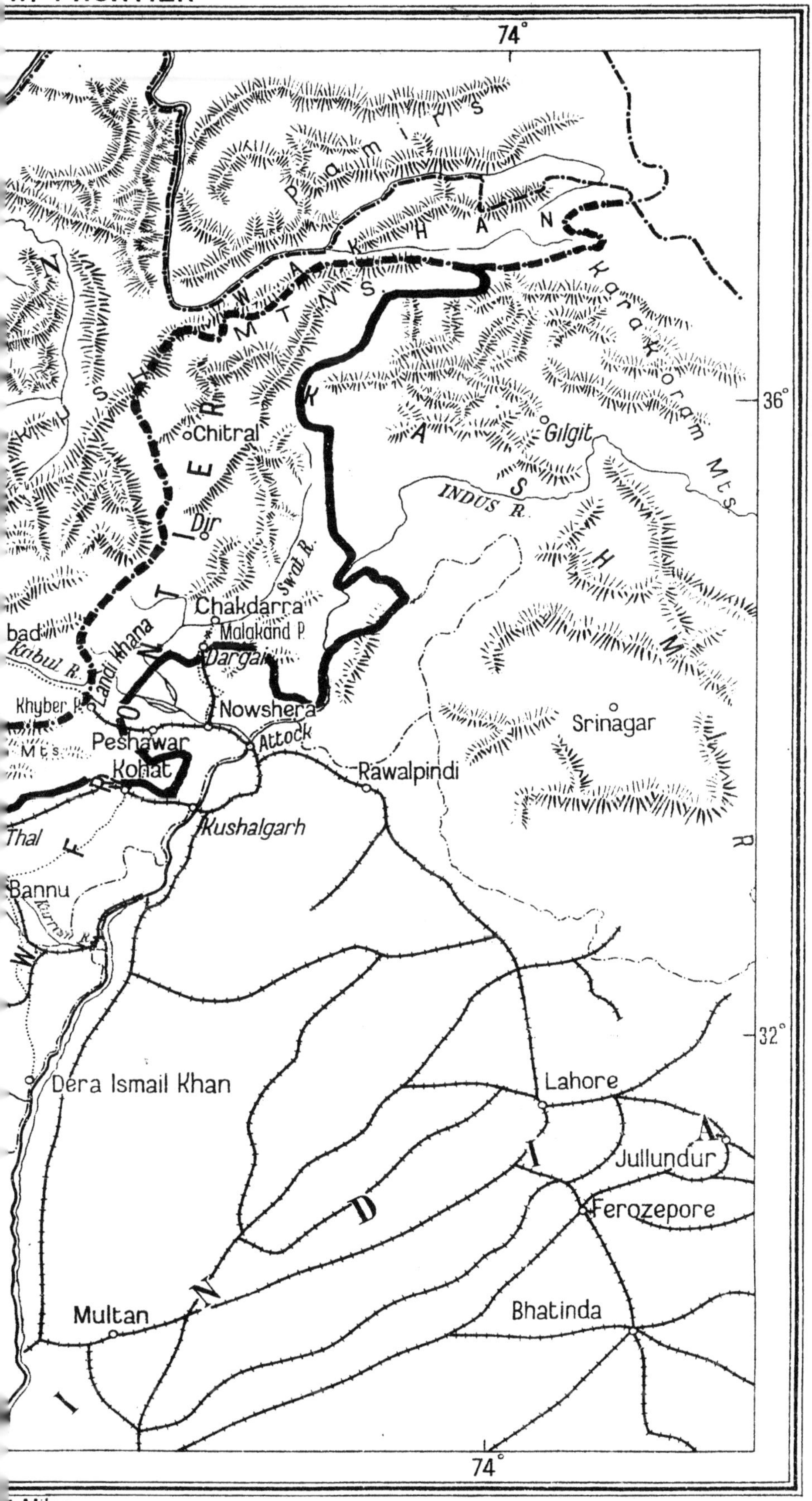
74°
Pamirs
KHAN
WAKHAN
MTNS
HINDU KUSH
Karakoram Mts.
36°
Chitral
Gilgit
KASHMIR
INDUS R.
Dir
Swat R.
Chakdarra
Malakand P.
Landi Khana
Dargai
bad
Kabul R.
Khyber P.
Nowshera
Srinagar
Peshawar
Attock
Mts.
Kohat
Rawalpindi
Kushalgarh
Thal
N.W. FRONTIER
Bannu
Kurram R.
32°
Lahore
Dera Ismail Khan
INDIA
Jullundur
Ferozepore
Multan
Bhatinda
74°

4 Miles 100 150 Miles

GENERAL STAFF INDIA.

Helio. S.I.O. Dehra Dun.

www.ingramcontent.com/pod-product-compliance
Ingram Content Group UK Ltd.
Pitfield, Milton Keynes, MK11 3LW, UK
UKHW051128260726
13967UKWH00010B/2921